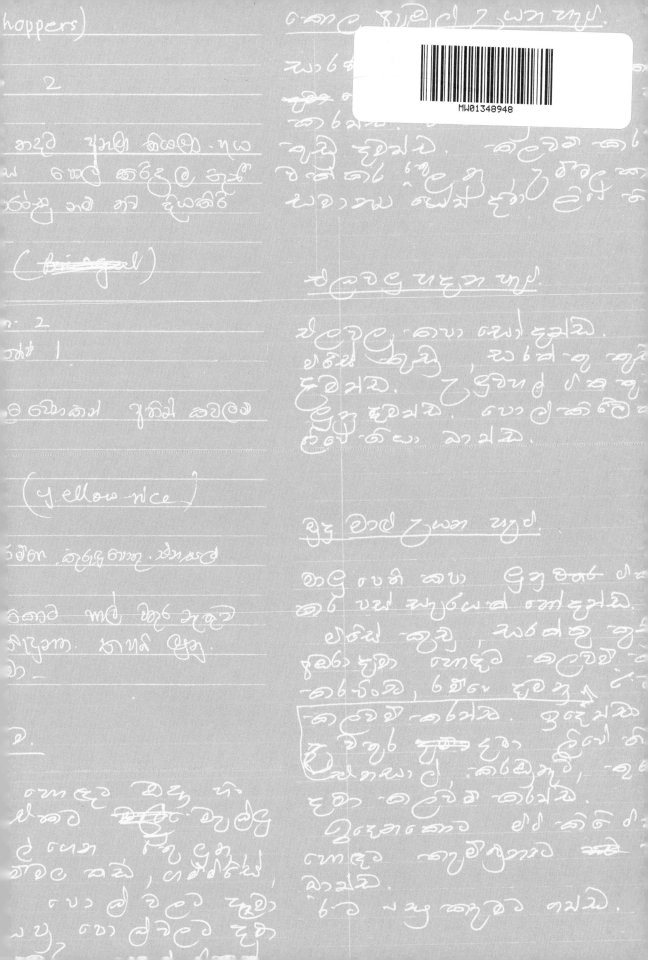

ජයන්ති

අභ්‍යාස පොත

විෂය	Milk,
නම	Spice
පන්තිය	& Curry
පාසැල	Leaves

ඡ 5   148 x 210 මි. මී

පිටු 40   මිල රු. 1·45

ජ. අ. පො. ති

Milk, Spice & Curry Leaves

Hill Country Recipes from the Heart of Sri Lanka

RUWANMALI SAMARAKOON-AMUNUGAMA

Food photography by DL ACKEN

Copyright © 2020 by Ruwanmali Samarakoon-Amunugama
Cover and interior studio food photography copyright © 2020 by DL Acken
For information on all other photos see page 179.

All rights reserved. No part of this publication may be reproduced, stored in a retrieval system, or transmitted in any form or by any means, electronic, mechanical, photocopying, recording, or otherwise, without the prior written permission of the publisher.
For more information, contact the publisher at:
TouchWood Editions
Touchwoodeditions.com

The information in this book is true and complete to the best of the author's knowledge. All recommendations are made without guarantee on the part of the author or the publisher.

Edited by Lesley Cameron
Design by Tree Abraham
Illustrations on pages 40 and 41 by Tree Abraham

Cataloguing information available from Library and Archives Canada
ISBN: 9781771513296 (hardcover)
ISBN: 9781771513302 (ebook)

TouchWood Editions gratefully acknowledges that the land on which we live and work is within the traditional territories of the Lkwungen (Esquimalt and Songhees), Malahat, Pacheedaht, Scia'new, T'Sou-ke and W̱SÁNEĆ (Pauquachin, Tsartlip, Tsawout, Tseycum) peoples.

We acknowledge the financial support of the Government of Canada through the Canada Book Fund, and the province of British Columbia through the Book Publishing Tax Credit.

This book was produced using FSC®-certified, acid-free papers, processed chlorine free, and printed with soya-based inks.

Printed in China

24 23 22 21 20   1 2 3 4 5

For my grandparents
Leelawathi Kumarihamy Kiridena and
Mudiyanselage Herath Banda Samarakoon

Contents

- 9 INTRODUCTION
- 15 THE ESSENCE OF SRI LANKAN COOKING
- 21 THE PILLARS
- 33 TIPS AND OTHER THINGS TO KNOW
- 47 RECIPES
  - 49 Grains
  - 63 Vegetable Dishes
  - 89 Fruit, Nut, and Lentil Dishes
  - 109 Meat and Poultry Dishes
  - 123 Seafood Dishes
  - 133 Salads
  - 149 Mallum, Sambol, and Pickles
  - 159 Small Bites with Tea
  - 165 Beverages
- 177 ACKNOWLEDGEMENTS
- 179 PHOTO CAPTIONS
- 180 INDEX

View of the Temple of the Holy Tooth and Library from across the Lake, Kandy, Ceylon.

INTRODUCTION

"Their entire life-style is different; those in the villages living a simple uncomplicated life free from the hustle and bustle of traffic, in a fresh and clean atmosphere ..."
(Doreen Alles, *Traditional Foods & Cookery Down the Ages*)

The Road from Colombo to Peradeniya

Sri Lanka is one of the most breathtaking places in the world, and no matter how often I go back, I never cease to be amazed by the incredible geography and flora and fauna of this island. Some of my fondest memories of my family's numerous visits to Sri Lanka from Canada over the years are of the many road trips we took with my extended family of uncles, aunts, and cousins. I can recall as a child being in awe of how much one region differed from the next. This was especially true as we travelled several hours by car from the capital city of Colombo to my grandmother's house (and the home my mother grew up in) in Peradeniya, Kandy.

As a child sitting in the back seat, I would watch the remarkable transition from bustling Colombo city life with its open shops and street vendors to slow-paced village life in Peradeniya. I witnessed the drastic transition in landscape from Colombo's western coastline to the lush, cool hill country of Sri Lanka's Central Province. Set amid hills on a plateau high in the south-central wet zone, Kandy is part of the Central Highlands, a region that is home to some of the country's highest mountains. On the drive from Colombo to Kandy, I would see the ocean, flat grassy fields, waterfalls, river gorges, and tall forested mountains, all within the span of only a few hours.

Our usual route always included a break to eat hot lump rice (rice and curries wrapped in banana leaves) at a local rest house, followed by a detour to Nuwara Eliya for tea. My mother was ever-vigilant as we made our way along the narrow roads that snake around the edges of high slopes, but my eyes would be on the vast estates of finely cultivated tea. From a distance the tea pickers appeared as scattered specks of brilliant colour—wind-strewn flowers against terraces of green. And along the hillsides, local farmers stood by stalls, displaying their harvests for sale: jackfruits, leeks, carrots, cabbage, potatoes, beets, avocados, mangos, and papayas. After briefly stopping to pick up fruits for the following morning's breakfast, we would drive to our favourite tea house, nestled in the cool misty hills. There we would sip our cups of hot black tea, as fresh as the surroundings and equally satisfying.

Hill Country

We would arrive late in the evening at my grandmother's house, and I would awaken the following morning to birdsong. I would find my mother already dressed, eating breakfast and chatting with family or friends who had dropped in. This summed up Peradeniya for me: happy, informal reunions around delicious meals. In later years my grandmother cooked less, but the household help that had been with her for almost their entire lives were well versed in her recipes. They prepared local varieties of rice, *pittu* (steamed rice flour rolls), *aapa* (bowl-shaped rice flour pancakes), coconut *sambol* and *roti*, and green leafy *mallum* (finely cut greens), as well as typical hill country curries such as jackfruit, beetroot, pumpkin, and ash plantain. For afternoon tea, my sister and I would go to our aunt and uncle's house next door, happily anticipating the homemade cakes and sweet treats.

Almost every visit to my mother's hometown included a day trip to Peradeniya's Royal Botanical Gardens and joining evening crowds at the annual Perahara festival in Kandy. In between family gatherings and sightseeing, we made trips into town to places such as the Kandy Central Market to find freshly picked fruits and vegetables, meats, fresh and dried fish, bottled palm oils, and ground and whole spices. The stunning displays of spices stacked on top of tables or piled in baskets offered an unparalleled array of scents and colours.

Although the pace of life is slow in my mother's hometown, our visits seemed to go by quickly. Before leaving Peradeniya, however, we would make a trip to my father's home village in the neighbouring Western Province. My paternal grandfather originally cultivated various coconut, fruit, and paddy (rice) plantations in the Central and Western Provinces. Physically being in the place that my father told me so much about when I was growing up in Canada always felt surreal. Quietly stepping foot on the land and looking across acres of coconut trees brought to life the stories about my grandfather. I would invariably recall my father's words, that my grandfather had started it all with just one coconut plant.

Developing a Taste for Hill Country Recipes

The memories and experiences of our travels as a family inspired me to maintain a connection to our heritage. My parents fostered our Sri Lankan traditions throughout my childhood in Canada, but there was one part of our culture that I was particularly drawn to: the food. The simple act of preparing the dishes and sharing them with family and friends felt natural to me. Just as I enjoyed travelling and taking in the small details of a scene or landscape, I equally enjoyed the quiet intricacies of cooking. Watching my mother cook the various foods we had in Sri Lanka, and seeing how the meals brought people together, became a strong part of my connection to our culture.

Often at my mother's side in the kitchen, I found myself paying close attention to her recipes—and the stories she attached to them. Unconsciously paying homage to my parents, grandparents, and our shared heritage, I learned about the ingredients my grandfathers cultivated and my grandmothers cooked with. Cooking with my mother also encouraged me to develop my own culinary instinct (since she, like most all Sri Lankan cooks, rarely measured spices or ingredients). While we did not always have the specific cooking tools or exact ingredients called for in the original recipes, the dishes were always so flavourful.

The majority of the recipes in this book originate from the hill country and are village-style curries the way my grandmother used to make them, while still several other recipes reflect the country's diverse and impressive regional foods. Naturally, most all recipes feature flavours or methods that are a result of historic culinary influences to Sri Lanka (originated from Portuguese, Dutch, and British colonial times).

The first section of the book, "The Essence of Sri Lankan Cooking," shares the basic principles of what is commonly known to Sri Lankans as their rice and curry diet. "The Pillars" discusses the three chief ingredient categories central to Sri Lankan cooking: coconut, rice, and spices. Recipes for roasted and unroasted curry powder are also provided—these are my family's recipes.

The section "Tips and Other Things to Know" includes information about using key spices and ingredients, traditional cooking methods, and the texture and consistency of dishes. This is followed by a recipe section, and several of the recipes include tips on how to save time as well as suggestions for menu planning.

Every Sri Lankan meal I make gives me a renewed appreciation for my upbringing and heritage. And inviting family and friends to share the meals I grew up with lets me extend the same generosity I experienced on my many travels in Sri Lanka. With this book, I invite you to develop your culinary instinct for Sri Lankan cooking, and to share the meals you make with family and friends.

14

THE ESSENCE OF SRI LANKAN COOKING

"Despite a complex blend of spices, Sri Lankan dishes are simple to prepare."
(Douglas Bullis and Wendy Hutton, *The Food of Sri Lanka*)

There is an art to Sri Lankan cooking: an intentional blending of plants and spices and a careful balancing of fats, acids, starches, proteins, and grains. The use of the freshest ingredients, the harmonization of various textures and consistencies, and the characterization of dishes by their vivid colour and rich aroma: this is the essence of Sri Lankan cuisine, and these are the factors the cook instinctively considers when preparing any dish.

Some aspects of Sri Lankan cooking have remained unchanged across the generations. For example, Sri Lankans tend to refer to their diet as the "rice and curry" diet. In contrast to a course-based menu, a main grain and several complementary dishes are brought to the table together. The types of dishes served depends on the main dish, but usually there is a meat or fish dish, two to three vegetable and fruit dishes, and a lentil dish. The grain is usually the largest in proportion to other dishes. Curries and other dishes are not overly large in quantity. This variety allows for a well-balanced meal and an equilibrium of flavours (spicy and cool), consistencies (dry, which is usually the texture of the grain, and moist, which is provided by the gravies of the curries), and textures (soft, hard, and fibrous meats, fruits, and vegetables). For dessert, generally a variety of fresh fruits are served, and on more formal occasions, traditional desserts, which tend to be very sweet and rich, make an appearance. Beverages play a key part to aid digestion and enhance the flavours of a meal or dessert. (You will find that a Sri Lankan rarely serves dessert without the satisfying accompaniment of a hot tea!)

The cooking methods of village cooks and past generations have also left their mark on the cuisine. My late grandmother's home in Peradeniya sits on a property that you wish only to walk barefoot upon. It once had an open well for bathing, vegetable and flower gardens, and papaya and coconut trees. The kitchen has two open entrances (one leading to the back garden), an open hearth with utensils hanging overhead, and earthen clay pots. Growing up, I would listen to my mother recount stories of my grandmother's cooking: she made a jackfruit curry that simmered in a *walang* (a large unglazed clay pot) on a low, open flame overnight; prepared her own ginger preserves from the large gingerroot unearthed from her garden; made ghee with fresh milk from the family's cows; and cooked with the coconuts collected from her own trees. She would prepare *sambols* with a *miris gala*, a tool made of stone that would by today's standards be considered an artifact. Ingredients would be placed on the stone base of the *miris gala* (literally, chili stone) and ground by rolling a cylindrical stone over top. This *miris gala* is still used in the house in Peradeniya, along with the *vangediya* and *mol gaha* (picture a gargantuan mortar and pestle). My grandmother had two sets of *vangediya* and *mol gaha*: one wooden, to pound raw rice paddy into rice flour, and one stone, to grind spices.

My mother recalls that beef and poultry were prepared infrequently and were more of a treat (partly because my grandmother was Buddhist and didn't eat meat). Beetroot, potato, snake gourd, bitter gourd, pumpkin, and eggplant (commonly called *brinjal* in Sri Lanka), however, were just a few of the many vegetables, either gathered from the market or purchased from a vendor travelling through villages, carrying fresh fruits and vegetables.

The diet of those living in the Central Province was greatly influenced by the natural environment: chilly and crisp at higher elevations, such as Nuwara Eliya, with spring-like conditions in Kandy on the same day. A weather pattern characteristic to Sri Lanka is alternating wet and dry spells with seasonal monsoons. Yala, the southwest monsoon, occurs from May to August and brings heavy rain to the south-central interior and southwestern region. These two areas comprise the "wet zone" and offer perfect conditions for growing tea, rice, and an abundance of fruits, tubers, and vegetables. (Maha, the gentler northeast monsoon, occurs from October to January and brings rain to the north. Most of the southeast, east, and northern parts of the country comprise the "dry zone.")

Many of the stories about my grandmother refer to her hospitality. In addition to raising seven children, she opened her home to almost daily visits from friends and extended family, so she ensured there was always enough food to serve her family and guests. She also regularly took food to her neighbours and the nearby temple. Her generosity nurtured values around the importance of family and community.

When my mother immigrated to Ontario, Canada, in the mid-1970s she brought these ideals and values with her. She showed me from a young age that food is much more than something to be swallowed on the go or unthinkingly consumed at set times of the day. Rather, mealtime is to be appreciated, celebrated, shared, and most importantly, enjoyed! It is a time for the family to take a break, to gather together and relax in each other's company. On more formal occasions, meals served Sri Lankan–style are works of art, showcasing hospitality and abundance.

Despite not having all the traditional cooking tools—or even the exact ingredients—my mother mastered the art of Sri Lankan cooking in a Western kitchen. She adapted a mix of contemporary and traditional cooking methods to make everything from comforting chicken curry and my sister's favourite devilled potatoes to her fancy yellow rice topped with fried cashews and raisins. On special occasions, she made milk rice, and for weekend road trips, she made my father's much-loved rice and curries packed in banana leaves.

The recipes I have included in this collection are some of my personal favourites. They are old family recipes with fond memories attached to them. I have included information I deem most important for creating a good Sri Lankan dish, using ingredients readily available in North America. It is with joy that I have been able to make these recipes for my own husband and daughter, and I hope you too will take time to delight in the varied and layered flavours of Sri Lankan cooking.

Fig. 63.—*Corypha umbraculifera* of Ceylon (after Ransonnet).

THE PILLARS

"The main substance with which they fill their bellies is rice, the other things are but to give it a relish."
(Robert Knox, *An Historical Relation of the Island Ceylon In the East-Indies*)

Essential Ingredients

Coconut and Coconut Milk (*Pol* and *Pol Kiri*)
The image of lofty coconut trees waving to and fro in the wind is almost synonymous with Sri Lanka. As idyllic as this image is, their main role on the island is a functional one. Coconut is usually featured in every meal of the day, whether in the form of fresh, dried, or roasted flesh, or liquid oil or milk.

Fresh coconut is used in the preparation of traditional grain dishes such as *pittu* and accompaniments such as *sambol* and *mallum*; while sprinklings of dry or roasted coconut are added as thickening agents to meat curries and dessert toppings. Coconut milk is the traditional thickening agent and gravy base for curries, and it helps to balance the flavours and cool the heat of chili.

I still recall my father using a *hiramanaya*, a traditional manual tool used to scrape out the white meat of a coconut. After cutting a fresh coconut in half and saving its water, he would hold one half of the coconut against the head of the scraper (its base clamped to the side of the table or countertop) and use his other hand to circle the crank to rotate the serrated metal head, grinding the fruit into a fine snow-like pile. It was a time-consuming process, but the fresh coconut (and coconut *sambol* that resulted) were worth the labour. Many of the *mallum* and *sambol* recipes in this book call for scraped or grated coconut. For these recipes, you want finely grated coconut and you may use fresh, dessicated, or frozen (see page 34 for more information).

But perhaps the most important part of coconut in Sri Lankan cooking is coconut milk—the liquid that comes from the pressed meat of a coconut. Sri Lanka's time-honoured rice dish *kiri bath* (literally, milk rice) is traditionally prepared with rich coconut milk. Both of my grandmothers prepared their own coconut milk by scraping the fresh coconut meat, soaking it in water, and then pressing up to five extracts of milk, the first extract being the thickest.

Coconut milk is a principal ingredient for almost all Sri Lankan curries and pulls together the spices and other ingredients. Furthermore, it helps balance flavours, soften proteins, neutralize acids, and reduces the heat of chili. For the curry recipes in this book, you will require *unsweetened* coconut milk, so its flavour, while distinct, is only mildly sweet. Canned coconut milk is widely available in grocery stores, but make sure to read the label to distinguish the unsweetened from the condensed/sweetened varieties, as well as from coconut cream (sometimes used when thick coconut milk is required). Some labels will also indicate if the milk is light in fat or flavour. As brands may yield modestly different results, try out a few to learn which ones work best for different recipes. Many of the recipes in this book use 3 tablespoons to ¼ cup of coconut milk; others require slightly more coconut milk, and some require a bit of water to be added to thin the milk. If you are adding more coconut milk to a recipe to thicken it, do so about 1 tablespoon at a time, allow the milk to simmer and blend into the curry, then taste again.

If you do not have coconut milk on hand, homogenized full fat cow's milk may sometimes be used as a substitute. This is the case for dal curry, and some vegetable curries. Where cow's milk is an acceptable substitute for coconut milk, it will be listed in the ingredients.

Rice (*Bath*)

It is common for rice to be served at every meal of the day, even in some desserts. Some examples of ground rice (or rice flour) dishes are *pittu* (steamed rice flour rolls often served at breakfast), *aappa* or hoppers (bowl-shaped rice flour pancakes), and *idiappan* or string hoppers (rice flour that has been made into a mixture and is then pressed into strings and shaped into lattice-like coaster sized mats). To make authentic, traditional *pittu*, *aapa*, and string hoppers you need specialized utensils not readily available in North America.

There are countless varieties of rice produced throughout the world that range in shape, colour, aroma, texture, and nutritional content (whole grain, short grain, pearl, broken, parboiled, raw, country, sticky, etc.). Some varieties have specific names—such as *samba*, jasmine, or basmati—that indicate the origin or locality of the rice. *Samba* and *suduru samba*, for example, are varieties of small-grain table rice produced in Sri Lanka and are favoured choices among locals. Perhaps the most obvious difference between rice varieties is their colour, such as white, brown, and red. Rice varieties fall into two categories: milled and unmilled. Milled, or "polished," rice appears white because the outer husk of bran is removed during the production process. Un-milled rice appears red or brown because the husk has been retained. It is the most nutritious rice, and it is the healthier choice for people with diabetes, in particular.

Try different kinds of rice to find out what flavours appeal most to your family. For example, white jasmine rice has a light scent that goes well with spicy or complex curry flavours. Part of what makes it sticky is its starch content—it and other types of milled rice are high in starch. In contrast, brown rice is more fibrous because most of its bran is retained; therefore, it is healthier than white rice. The darker the colour of the rice, the higher its nutritional value. Brown rice complements hearty vegetables, *mallums*, meat and dal curries. For many of the curries in this book, basmati rice is a nice complement. The milder, slightly nutty aroma of basmati rice brings out the earthy flavours of curry leaves, *pandanus* leaves, and spices. Basmati rice is widely available in Asian food stores and larger chain grocery stores.

It is good practice to wash rice under cold, running water until the water runs clear to remove excess starch or loose particles prior to cooking. In Sri Lankan villages some people still use a special concave vessel called a *nambiliya* for washing rice. Its many grooves hold back the small stones and debris as the grains of rice are washed clean. I still recall my mother using hers in Canada when I was a child.

Cooking rice very much depends on the variety of rice and the container you are using to cook the rice. While the general rule of thumb for cooking white rice is the 1:2 ratio of 1 cup rice to 2 cups water, the amount of water and the cooking time required may vary. For this reason, it is always advisable to follow the directions provided on the packaging. Whether cooking the rice on the stovetop, or in an electric or microwave rice cooker, it is better to start with a little less water and then add more water during the cooking process. (Too much water will give you mushy or clumpy rice; too little will give you hard rice.) It is advisable for 1 cup rice to start with 1½ cups water, either in a rice cooker or on the stove, and then increase the water about ½ cup at a time, as required. Add salt to your taste.

Because rice expands as it cooks, be aware of how many cups of rice your pot or rice cooker is able to accommodate. (If you are using a rice cooker to cook for large groups, you may need one with a 20-cup capacity.) Too much rice in a small container may result in uneven cooking. Ideally, the rice grains should be unbroken and cooked through. Use a fork or wooden spoon to gently stir the rice during the cooking process, to undo lumps, and fluff it when cooking is complete. Avoid using metal spoons to stir rice during cooking as they will mush or break the grains. Use a spoon with a large broad head for serving.

Key Spices and Ingredients

Though I took for granted the astounding array of ingredients my mother used for cooking, her spice cabinet was a playground for a child's imagination. It contained an enchanting display of neatly stacked bottles filled with whole and ground spices with bright earthy colours: dark red, burnt orange, pale and golden yellows, auburn, and deep brown. I can still hear the "tick-tick" sound of the spoon hitting against the glass jar every time she eyeballed the exact amount of whatever particular spice she required. This is the way with Sri Lankan cooks; they never use measuring utensils of any sort, but rather something even more precise: their instinct.

Many of the items in this section are basic ingredients in Sri Lankan cooking that grow wild and abundantly throughout the island. Fortunately, these days South Asian spices and ingredients are increasingly available in North American supermarkets, Asian, and ethnic food stores, as well as farmers' markets, making it easier to recreate the unique characteristics of Sri Lanka's hill country dishes and their tropical, rustic, earthy flavours.

An A to Z of Essential Flavourings

Cardamom (*Enasal*)
Cardamom is the seed of a tropical fruit in the ginger family, Zingiberaceae, that is grown extensively in Sri Lanka. It has a warm, spicy-sweet flavour with an intensely aromatic fragrance. The delicate seed pods of cardamom are harvested when they are green and then sun-dried. Enclosed in the pods are several tiny black seeds, which may be extracted, but in most recipes the whole pods are used. Cardamom is commonly used in rice dishes, meat or fish curries, desserts, and spiced tea.

Chili Pepper (*Miris*)
Hot chili—or hot pepper—from the Solanaceae family, is practically synonymous with Asian and Indian cooking. There are many kinds of chili peppers, ranging in colour, shape, and size, which allows for a variety of uses. Unripened chilies are usually green; mature chilies can range from light green, yellow, and orange to dark red. Then there are the very small, thin red or bird's eye chilies that are extremely hot. But it is a misconception to think that red chilies are hot and green mild. Most of the curry recipes in this book call for either cayenne powder (made from dried and crushed red chilies) as well as Thai and/or Indian green chilies. (Thai and Indian green chilies appear very similar to one another and either of these varieties works for the recipes.) Dried chili flakes are usually fried first to release their aroma, after which other ingredients are added.

Ground paprika, made from a variety of mild and sometimes sweet peppers, is used in combination with cayenne powder for many recipes in this book, primarily for its brilliant colour and when a milder taste is desired.

Another pepper used in a few of the recipes is banana peppers (called *malu miris* in Sinhalese and also often referred to as capsicum in Sri Lanka and widely used in cooking). These long peppers are yellowish-green in colour. They are very mild, so they are not used in the preparation of curries. Because of their roomy cavity, they are often stuffed with a savoury filling and fried, or fried in a bit of oil on their own, and sometimes added to salads. The thick large round bell capsicum peppers may be used in salads or for a garnish.

Cinnamon (*Kurundu*)
The cinnamon tree is an evergreen tree of the Lauraceae family. True cinnamon is native to Sri Lanka and is ranked as being of the highest quality in the world. Cinnamon is the delicately fragrant orange bark of the tree, and cinnamon sticks are the dried curls of bark, which are removed in thin shavings. Cinnamon is extensively used in curries, sweets, and sometimes in tea and medicinal drinks.

Cloves (*Karabu nati*)
Cloves are the dried, unopened flower buds of a tropical evergreen tree called *Eugenia caryophyllus*, from the Myrtaceae family. The buds are pale in

colour at first, then gradually turn green and later red, at which point they are ready for picking. Dried cloves may be used either whole or ground but always sparingly, as their pungent taste can dominate other flavours. Their sweet, spicy flavour lends itself well to curries, rice dishes, desserts, sweet meats, and teas.

Coriander Seeds (*Kothamalli*)
Coriander is a member of the Apiaceae family. Also commonly called cilantro when its fresh version is being referred to, it is an annual herb. While the entire plant is edible and widely used in cooking all over the world, only the seeds are normally used in Sri Lankan cooking. They are either finely ground or powdered and included in curry powders.

Curry Leaves (*Karapincha*)
Curry leaves are a member of the Rutaceae family and are a must in Sri Lankan cooking, but despite their name, they do not taste like curry spice. They come from a small evergreen tree called a curry tree (or *Murraya koenigii*), which grows abundantly in Sri Lanka's forests. Curry leaves are used both fresh and dried, but the aroma of the fresh is far superior. (In Sri Lanka fresh leaves are regularly used because of their availability.) They have a distinctive flavour and are added to most curries, dals, savoury filled snacks, and some rice dishes. Usually the leaves are first *tempered* in oil (see page 42), onion and/or mustard seeds are then added before all the other ingredients. Other times, fresh leaves are ripped into small pieces and added directly to curries. Both of these methods help to release and enhance the flavour of the curry leaves. For a single curry, four to eight leaves are generally used, although sometimes an entire sprig is used.

Fennel Seeds (*Maduru*)
Part of the Apiaceae family, these seeds look like cumin seeds and can be confused with aniseed because they have a similar, though slightly milder sweet aniseed (liquorice) taste. The seeds are ground for use in curry powder.

Fenugreek Seeds (*Uluhaal*)
Fenugreek seeds are the very small flat square-shaped yellow-brown seeds of a bean-like plant from the family Leguminosae or Fabaceae. They have a slightly bitter flavour and are largely used as a thickener, which can be enhanced with overnight soaking. Only a little is added to curries and *kiri hodhi* (white coconut milk gravy).

Ginger (*Inguru*)
Widely used in Asian cooking, the ginger plant belongs to the Zingiberaceae family. Young ginger-root is juicy and fleshy and has a mild taste, while mature gingerroot is fibrous and has a very pungent sweet taste. In Sri Lankan cooking, the thin finger-like variety is used either fresh or ground in curries, chutneys, pickles, desserts, sweets, home remedies, and tea.

***Goraka*—also called Garcinia cambogia (*Goraka*)**
Goraka or *garcinia gummi-gutta* is a tropical species of Garcinia.

Goraka is the fruit borne from a tropical evergreen tree, the *goraka* tree, abundant in the forests of western Sri Lanka. The fruit is bright orangish-red and segmented and is commonly used for its acidic properties and sometimes as a thickening agent. When the fruit is ripe it is dried and stored, which turns its colour to black. In Sri Lanka, it is sold in markets in the form of dried segments. For use in cooking, the dried pieces are stored in salted brine and kept in the fridge. *Goraka* is used in the preparation of pork and fish curries and the pieces are removed before serving. Although this ingredient may not be available in North America, *goraka* paste can be found in Asian food stores. Tamarind paste and sometimes lemon juice may be used as a substitute, and in those cases their equivalents are noted in recipes.

Lemon Grass (*Sera*)
Lemon grass is part of the Poaceae (formerly Gramineae) family. It is a tall, coarse tropical grass native to Sri Lanka and is widely used in Asian cooking. Its fresh leaves and stalk contain an essential oil also present in lemon peel; it therefore has a very strong and dominating lemony flavour and is only used in small quantities in Sinhalese cuisine. Only the lower white bulbous part of the

stalk (the bottom 4 to 6 inches of the vegetable) is used for cooking, either dried or fresh. It is sliced or pounded and added to beef or prawn curries and soups.

Maldives Fish (*Umbalakada*)
Maldives fish is another distinguishing ingredient of Sri Lankan cooking and one of the main exports from the Maldives to Sri Lanka. Maldives fish is bonito, a variety of tuna, that has been completely dried, smoked, and then either finely ground or powdered. The flavour is very strong and can be dominating, so care must be taken not to add too much to a dish. Flakes are added to *sambols*, but never to curries. Though it may take some searching, you may be able to find this product in Asian food stores. There is no substitute for this ingredient.

Mustard (*Aba*)
Mustard seeds, from the Brassicaceae (formerly Cruciferae) family, come in yellow, brown, and black varieties. Black and brown mustard seeds have a sharp, pungent taste, while yellow mustard seeds are milder. Mustard seeds are used in the preparation of certain meat, fish, and vegetable curries, *mallums*, and *sambols*. Both the yellow and black varieties are used in cooking, but the black are more commonly used in Sri Lankan recipes. Whole seeds are often "popped" in hot oil to release their flavour. Other times they are finely ground for use in curry powders or pickles.

Pandan/Pandanus Leaf or Screw Pine (*Rampe*)
There are numerous varieties of the pandanus plant, which belong to the Pandanaceae (screw pine) family, all varying in size and appearance. The stiff, flat green blade-like leaf is widely used in Sri Lankan cooking for its distinctive nutty scent. Dry, frozen, or fresh pieces of the leaf are usually tempered with other ingredients (e.g., onion, curry leaves) or added directly to meat curries and rice dishes. The leaf is tough and fibrous and therefore removed before serving. Fresh *pandanus* is sometimes available in Asian food stores. There is no substitute for this ingredient, but you can omit it from the curries that call for it if you cannot find it, as the overall flavour will not be hindered. Its absence from rice dishes will be noticeable, although they too may be made without it.

Pepper (*Gammiris*)
Black and white peppercorns belong to the Piperaceae family and are the berries of the pepper plant, which is a climbing vine. The berries grow in clusters and are green when unripe and red when mature. Black peppercorns are actually unripe green berries that have been sun-dried after harvesting, which turns them black. White peppercorns are the seeds of mature red berries that have been soaked in water for a few days. The soaking causes the flesh of the berry to rot. The seeds are washed clean of any flesh and then sun-dried. Black pepper is added to curries, rice dishes and is sometimes used as a substitute for chili. White pepper is used less often and has a milder taste.

Tamarind (*Siyambala*)
Tamarind is the fruit of the tropical tamarind tree that belongs to the Leguminosae or Fabaceae family. The fruit are actually seed pods that have a brown casing and look like misshapen, swollen string beans. Tamarind is the soft, fleshy, acidic pulp inside the pod that covers the hard, dark brown seeds. Though not widely used in Sinhalese cuisine, it is sometimes used in the preparation of certain meat curries for its acidic properties.

Turmeric (*Kaha*—literally, yellow)
Turmeric belongs to the ginger family, Zingiberaceae. Sometimes confused with saffron, turmeric root is cured, dried, and powdered or ground. It does not have much flavour but is included in many curries for its purifying effects and especially for its brilliant yellow colour, which is desirable for white curries, lentil dishes, and yellow rice.

The Spices of Curries

Achieving the right colour is essential to creating a visually appealing curry, one that will whet the appetite. A curry's colour provides people with a sense of its flavour, even before they have had an opportunity to taste it. The colour of a curry has much to do with the marriage of spice and coconut milk, and hints at the cooking method used. In fact, the colour is so significant that, in Sri Lanka, curries are usually referred to (and characterized or classified) by their colour: red (*rathu*), black (*kalu*), and white (*suthu*). Spices release their flavours and aromas over different times, and the colour of a curry may deepen as it cooks. If the spices are very fresh, they yield a brighter colour and more pronounced flavours.

"Red" curries (and other "red" dishes) get their colour from dried and crushed whole red chilies or cayenne (chili powder) and, in recent years, ground paprika. In my grandmother's time, paprika was not used in cooking—it was not even available in Sri Lanka. The redness of a dish came from the addition of chilies. Although some Sri Lankan cooks still opt not to use paprika, its use in combination with cayenne powder is now common to achieve the desired colour without the intensity of the heat. (For this reason, most of the recipes in this book use both paprika and cayenne powders.) There is a term in Sinhalese, *mirisata*, that is used to indicate when a curry is to be prepared the "spicy way." *Miris* curries and dishes are prepared with additional chilies. (The direct translation of the word miris is "chili.")

A "black" curry is actually dark brown in colour. The colour is due, in part, to the addition of roasted curry powder (made from whole spices that have been roasted and then finely ground), which has a colour similar to that of ground coffee. But not all recipes that call for roasted curry powder are "black" curries. This term is used when specific ingredients are roasted in a heated pan and then ground to make a powder called *kalu kudu*. Literally meaning "black powder," when this is simmered in a curry already containing roasted curry powder (such as pork curry), it results in a rich brown gravy. Roasted curry powder (see page 31) is generally used in the preparation of meat, and some dishes featuring fruits, such as jackfruit and cashew nut. Unroasted curry powder (see page 31) is used in the preparation of some vegetable, lentil, and fish dishes. These dishes exude a dark yellow to light golden-brown colour.

"White" curry dishes are so titled because they are prepared with an ample amount of coconut milk, a touch of turmeric, and little or no chili. (No chili is added when a white curry is prepared for children or seniors, but one can be used when prepared for a crowd.) White curries don't actually appear white; rather they are light yellow because of the addition of turmeric. Only vegetables and some fish are prepared in this manner because the mild flavour is preferred. White curries are usually finished with a splash of lime juice, which is essential to attaining the desired hint of sour.

Sinhalese unroasted curry powder is called *amu thuna paha* (literally, raw three-five). The name refers to the three to five spices that unroasted curry powder traditionally contains. The three essential spice seeds include cumin seeds, fennel seeds, and coriander seeds, and additionally curry leaves and/or pandanus leaves, and cinnamon bark. *Badupa thuna paha* (literally, roasted three-five) refers to the Sinhalese roasted curry powder used for meat, poultry, and some fruit dishes. Just about every family or generational recipe is different, with varying ratios of the essential three spice seeds (cumin seeds, fennel seeds, and coriander seeds) and differences in which additional spices (mustard seeds, peppercorns, chili, etc) are used for the roasted curry powder.

For the recipes in this book you will mostly require roasted curry powder (see page 31). There is no substitute for this. Unroasted curry powder, however, may be omitted—but do try making your own (see page 31). And have fun testing your own versions of both!

To prolong the freshness, flavour, and colour of spices, store them in airtight glass containers in a cool, dark place.

(Raw) Unroasted Curry Powder
Amu Thuna Paha Kudu

In a dry (not oiled) frying pan over low heat, lightly roast the cumin, fennel, and coriander seeds together just long enough to release their fragrance and remove any moisture. Shake the pan to roast the spices; you may also use a wooden spoon to stir continuously in the pan. Remove them from the pan and set aside to cool.

In the same pan over low heat (no need to clean the pan), dry-roast the curry leaves and cinnamon together for 2–3 minutes, until the curry leaves are crispy.

Let all the ingredients cool, and then put them into a spice or coffee grinder (this may have to be done in batches). Grind the spices to a fine powder. Spoon the curry powder into an airtight jar or container and store in a cool, dark space for up to 2 to 4 months.

Makes about 2 cups

½ cup cumin seeds (6 Tbsp)

¼ cup fennel seeds (4 Tbsp)

1½ cups coriander seeds (20–22 Tbsp)

20 fresh curry leaves (1½ sprigs)

2-inch Ceylon cinnamon stick, broken into small pieces

Roasted Curry Powder
Badupa Thuna Paha Kudu

Set a dry (not oiled) frying pan over high heat. When the pan is hot, add the rice. Watching the rice closely, heat it until the grains begin to pop. Shake the pan to help the grains roast evenly and to quicken the popping.

When the grains are evenly roasted and browned, pour them onto a plate or into a bowl and set aside to cool.

In the same pan (no need to clean it) over medium to medium-low heat, dry-roast separately the coriander seeds, cumin seeds, fennel seeds, cardamom seeds, cloves, and cinnamon pieces until a deep aroma is released and the spices are dark brown (but not burnt!). Shake the pan to roast the spices; you may also use a wooden spoon to stir continuously in the pan. As you brown each ingredient, pour them into a bowl and set aside.

In the same pan, dry-roast the curry leaves until crisped and browned. Add them to the bowl along with the roasted white rice.

Stir to combine all the roasted spices and spoon mixture into a spice or coffee grinder. (This may have to be done in batches.) Grind to a fine powder.

Spoon the roasted curry powder into an airtight jar or container and store in a cool, dark space for up to 2 to 4 months.

Makes about 2 cups

1–1½ Tbsp parboiled rice

½ cup cumin seeds (6 Tbsp)

¼ cup fennel seeds (4 Tbsp)

1½ cups coriander seeds (20–22 Tbsp)

¾ tsp green cardamoms (10 pods; use seeds only)

¾ tsp whole cloves (20)

2-inch Ceylon cinnamon stick, broken into pieces

20 fresh curry leaves (1½ sprigs)

TIPS AND OTHER THINGS TO KNOW

My mother spent years mastering the art of preparing rice and curry in a Western kitchen. Even though she was familiar with Asian and South Asian ingredients, learning how to purchase and use imported products required a degree of experimentation, and adapting certain cooking techniques to enhance the natural qualities and flavours of ingredients involved a little trial and error. This section draws on the lessons we learned so that you too can master the art of preparing rice and curries in a Western kitchen.

With today's busy lifestyles, it is common for many home cooks to have little time for food preparation and to forgo practising simple steps that go a long way toward improving the taste and nutritional value of a meal. But taking the time to connect with the food we feed ourselves, our families, and our friends is the secret ingredient that makes the hill country diet so comforting. With practice, you will find that certain foods and cooking methods can produce a more wholesome, flavourful meal.

Prepping for Cooking

Part of the reason Sri Lankan dishes can appear intimidating or hard to make in Western countries lies in the kinds of utensils traditionally used in their preparation. Even the physical structure of a traditional Sri Lankan kitchen, particularly in rural areas, is different from a Western one. Traditional Sri Lankan cookware includes clay pots for making curries; grinding stones for grinding spices and preparing side or relish-like dishes; coconut shell spoons (*pol katu handi*) for cooking and serving; special moulds for pressing rice flour batter and frying foods; and special utensils for steaming grains and for grating coconut. These items are difficult to find even in specialty Asian markets in North America, but you can improvise with what is available.

For example, the recipes in this book are made using metal pots, saucepans, frying pans, and wooden spoons. (These are also good for simply avoiding scratching your pots and pans.) I recommend using a wide, medium-size stainless-steel, two-handled pot for curries that involve slow-cooking. Stainless-steel pots also work well for tempering ingredients (see page 42) as they conduct heat faster. Instead of hunting down a traditional coconut scraper for grating fresh coconut, you can use frozen grated coconut (fresh coconut that was previously scraped or grated and then frozen), which is available in the freezer aisle of Asian or Indian markets. Electric food choppers and electric spice or coffee grinders can be used to finely grind or chop ingredients (the key is to use a light touch when using them to chop leaves to avoid crushing and thereby altering their flavours), and mortars and pestles in varying sizes are widely available in department stores, specialty kitchen stores, and Asian markets. (A small to medium-size mortar and pestle will suffice for the recipes in this book.)

Try these tips for a more authentic experience:

- When cooking certain curries on the stovetop, combine ingredients without using a spoon. Lift the pot off the heat and, gripping it by its handles, gently move it in a figure-eight motion to combine and blend the coconut milk with the other ingredients. This is an assured way to avoid accidental breakage of tender or delicate ingredients (such as jackfruit and pineapple) through the use of metal spoons that may scrape the food or scratch the cooking vessel and even affect the flavour of the dish.
- When time permits, use a knife (instead of a chopper) to finely cut leaves or ingredients; use your hands to combine ingredients when coating meat with spices or when mixing sambols; and allow dishes, such as meat or jackfruit curries, that will benefit from longer cooking times, to cook for an hour or more. The taste will be ample reward for the wait.
- Familiarize yourself with nearby Asian markets to source spices and other ingredients, and take some time to visit your local farmers' markets—you're bound to find many varieties of fruits and vegetables (in particular, root and tuber vegetables, bulb vegetables, and peppers) there.
- You may find frozen grated coconut available in packets in the freezer aisle of South Asian markets; this is preferred for the recipes in this book. Alternatively, you may also try unsweetened desiccated coconut available in most all grocery stores in the baking aisle. When buying the desiccated variety, look for small light pieces (like snow) rather than long skinny threads. If you are using the frozen variety, thaw the coconut just to room temperature. If you are using desiccated coconut, re-hydrate it with a little water. Work the water into the coconut with your fingers, and microwave for 15–20 seconds. About a tablespoon of water to ¼ cup of coconut should do.

A further recipe for success, so to speak, is to take a bit of time to prepare yourself before you begin a recipe. Check the pantry to make sure you have all the spices, oil, and other key ingredients needed. Set out and prep those ingredients that may be left out at room temperature ahead of time. For example, something that was commonly kept and used in my grandmother's kitchens was a clay dish that had a cover and three or four compartments; in the compartments were turmeric root, curry powder, and chilies. This was kept handy and regularly topped up, as these three ingredients were almost always used. Preparing a plate of key ingredients (peeled and grated garlic and ginger, peeled and chopped onion, washed curry and *pandanus* leaves, etc.) just beforehand will help to make things easy.

Tips On Using Spices and Key Ingredients

Spices and spice powders are essential to the creation of all Sri Lankan dishes and curries. They impart those special flavours unique to South Asian cooking. The section "An A to Z of Essential Flavourings" has more information about those that are commonly used in Sri Lankan cooking and their individual flavours. But knowing how much to use is a skill that may be developed over time. Therefore, it is wise to begin with slightly less if you are still experimenting or learning your spice-level preference. Certain recipes call for the addition of whole spices such *pandanus* leaves or cinnamon sticks; these should be removed from dishes before serving. Some dishes call for the addition of curry leaves, cardamom, peppercorns, or cloves; these do not need to be removed prior to serving. Simply advise your guests to push them to the side of their plates.

The Cast
(Curry Leaves, Onion, Garlic, Ginger, Chilies)

These key ingredients lend Sri Lankan dishes their complex, layered flavours and are found in most curries. The idea is that this cast of flavours will balance each other, without any one of them overpowering another. Each cook may choose to use more or less of each to their liking, but for the recipes in this book these flavours are used in moderation.

Curry leaves are essential to Sri Lankan cooking. They are highly aromatic and impart a unique warm, nutty yet bright and distinctive flavour to the dishes they're being cooked in. Curry leaves are often sold in bags in the refrigerated aisles of Indian and Asian markets. The recipes in this book call for less than half a stem in most cases; however, if you are comfortable using curry leaves, you may add more to your liking. The leaves are either tempered (see page 42) first or ripped into small pieces and added directly to curries. Both methods help to release and enhance their flavour. Store curry leaves in your fridge in a sealed bag with the air pressed out. They will last for 2 to 3 weeks.

Onions are included in most savoury foods, including curries, *sambols*, and salads (*sambola*). Sri Lankan cooking makes use of a wide range of onions and the type that is used depends on the dish. Red onions have a sharper, more pronounced flavour, and are used in curries, *sambols*, and pickles. White onions are used in some curries (and curries prepared for children), dals, *sambols*, and salads.

The variety of red onions my grandmother used from the village she lived in were small in comparison to the size typically sold in North American grocery stores. If you happen upon the small, round red onions (not to be confused with shallots or pearl onions used in pickles) sometimes found in farmers' markets or Indian grocery stores, these work well for many of the recipes. Store onions in a cool, dry place.

Garlic and **ginger** are often used together. Typically, only a clove or two of fresh white garlic is needed. When using fresh ginger, break or slice off 1½ to 2 inches, and remove the peel. Most often garlic and ginger are finely grated or finely chopped; garlic can also be crushed using a mortar and pestle. These preparation techniques allow their pronounced flavours to melt into the sauce of the curry. They are a must for poultry or meat curries. It is also not uncommon to find a clove of garlic in some vegetable and or dal curries.

Select heads of garlic with wide, healthy cloves with no black spots and store them in a garlic pot or in a cool, dry place. If you are buying fresh ginger, look for plump roots without blemishes. If you do not need a large piece, just break off what you require and store the rest, unpeeled, in the fridge, wrapped in a paper towel. It should last for about 2 weeks.

The green **chilies** listed in the recipes refer to the small, thin, unripened green chilies that are often called Thai chilies and sometimes called Indian green chilies. This variety is very hot, so many of the recipes in this book call for only one, but Indian green chilies can be quite small, so you may want to add two of those. Chilies are either diagonally sliced in two and added to curries or very thinly sliced and added to *mallums*, *sambols*, or the filling of savoury filled snacks, such as pastries and patties. In Sri Lanka, it is not uncommon for one or two raw green chilies to be served directly on one's plate to be eaten with rice and curry.

Getting the Sour
(Lime, Goraka, Tamarind, Vinegar)

Like many Sri Lankans of her generation, my grandmother did not have a fridge. Given that Sri Lanka is a tropical country, one wonders what was used as a preservative in those times. The answer might lie in the common use of citric acids, such as lime, *goraka*, and tamarind, in cooking. Many Sri Lankan dishes have an element of sour in their flavour profile.

Lime juice is commonly used in upcountry cooking, perhaps originally because of its preservative properties. While it is used primarily because of its acidic properties, the distinctive flavour that lime imparts to a dish cannot be satisfactorily substituted with lemon, though this is done when lime is not on hand. The use of fresh lime juice as the finishing step for white curries, dals, coconut *sambols*, and salads is a must. Although only a small amount of lime juice is usually needed (just a squeeze of a wedge of lime—giving you about 1 teaspoon of juice—is added to a curry just before it is removed from the heat), there is no satisfactory substitute for its refreshing flavour that completes a dish. Similarly, salted lime pickle (*lunu dehi*) offers no relief from its tartness, so only a smidgen is served as a relish with a meal.

Fruit, meat, and fish dishes also include a sour dimension, some more modest than others. For certain recipes, such as young jackfruit curry (*polos ambula*) and sour fish (*malu ambul thiyal*), there is a more pronounced sourness. In fact, the Sinhala word *ambula* literally means sour. These particular recipes call for the addition of **goraka** (see pages 91, 119, 129). Dried pieces are brined in salted water or washed in hot water and either used whole or ground to a paste. If you are fortunate enough to find the dried pieces, brine them in a glass jar of water with a few tablespoons of salt and refrigerate. The pieces should last for several months. *Goraka* has a unique, pleasant sour taste and works as a tenderizer when added to meat dishes, such as black pork curry (see page 119).

Tamarind, though not as frequently used, is added in the preparation of some poultry, beef, gamey meat (such as lamb or mutton), or seafood.

Vinegar is added to a couple of the *badthum* recipes in this book, for salad dressings, and is the tangy base and preservative for vegetable pickles.

Preparing and Cutting Leaves, Fruits, and Vegetables for Curries and Salads

Presentation is part and parcel of Sri Lankan cooking, demonstrated in the uniform cutting of ingredients, the bright colour of dishes, the shaping of individual portions into geometric shapes, and the sprinkling of fried nuts and raisins atop dishes.

My grandmother said that how you cut a fruit, vegetable, or plant will affect its flavour. For this reason, my mother always took care in chopping chilies, plants, and herbs with a knife (rather than an electric chopper, as this can lead to a bitter taste), evenly cutting fruits and vegetables (whether they were to be fried, cooked in a curry, or mixed in a salad), cutting chilies and some vegetables on the diagonal, and cutting thin slices unless a coarser or chunkier shape was better suited to the dish. This was particularly exemplified in the cutting of beetroot and eggplant, and in the measured cutting of young jackfruit or pineapple into even, bite-size pieces. When pieces (whether meat, fruits, or vegetables) are cut uniformly, they cook evenly, are easy to pick up and eat, either with a fork or one's fingers (as Sri Lankans eat their meals with their fingers), and are easier to digest. Note, for many of the recipes, onions are finely chopped (almost to blend into the other ingredients of a dish or curry during cooking). Thicker slices tend to be used for fried dishes where the onion provides some texture and crunch.

Sri Lankans have also long incorporated the island's flora and fauna into their food. For example, banana leaves are used to parcel rice and curries, designed to be eaten on the go. They impart a subtle fragrance to the food and provide the ultimate environmentally friendly container. Here are a few key points to help you on your way as you prepare the recipes on the following pages.

Using Banana Leaves

You can find banana leaves at most Asian food stores. Before using them, wipe them with a damp cloth. If you plan on using them for packaging food or rice, gently swipe the leaves over a very hot element, allowing the surface and edges of each leaf to touch the element. You will hear some crackling and popping sounds. The purpose of heating the leaves is to soften and render them flexible so that they do not tear when wrapping, and to kill germs. Cut the leaves in half and cut the edges off.

To parcel rice and curries, tear/cut the banana leaves approximately the size of a rectangular place mat (12 inches by 16 inches). Place the leaf over a dinner plate to help you centre the placement of rice and curries. After you have finished spooning all the rice and curries onto the leaf, prepare to close the parcel by shifting the filled leaf on a slight diagonal. Hold a diagonal corner between your thumb and forefinger and bring it toward the centre. Fold the leaf over the rice and curries onto the leaf. Do the same with the opposing corner, almost like you are wrapping a gift. Pull together the remaining opposite two corners in same manner, while keeping the already closed corners pressed down. Quickly flip the bundle over to keep the sides from

opening. Use a torn thread of banana leaf to tie the parcel closed. If you will be freezing the parcel, you can wrap it in an additional layer of aluminum foil to help it keep its shape and to provide an extra layer of protection.

Using Curry Leaves

Pull the leaves upwards from the stem (begin at the bottom and push toward the tip) to release them. The stem and the leaves are full of essence, and the leaves are either used whole or ripped into small pieces. If a whole sprig is used, the stem is kept on. When first trying recipes, begin with the recipe's specified amount and gradually add more if you wish as you become more familiar with their flavour. Most Sri Lankan cooks will use a good portion of a sprig or a full sprig when cooking, but this is only recommended for those who are used to their flavour and cooking with them.

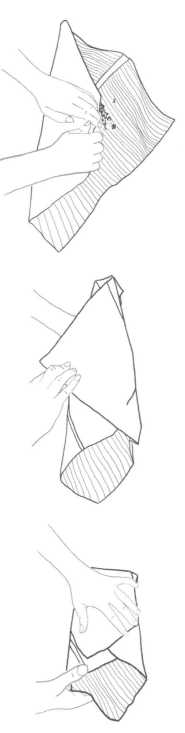

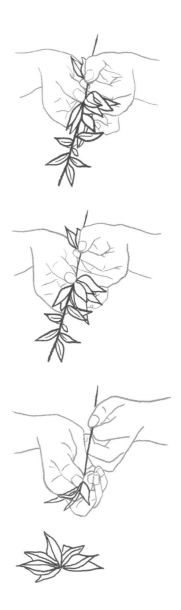

Cutting Mangoes

Place the mango on its side on a cutting board and slice the top or bottom tip off. Then you will be able to see where the nut is. Hold the side facing up with your palm pressed against it, slice across through the bottom side to cut one of the "cheeks" of the mango. Then carefully holding the mango again, sliced side up, cut the other cheek. Then carefully cut around the nut to slice the two remaining segments on the opposite sides. Slice each cheek in approximately three slices. Dice or slice as needed. Either use the nut for cooking or suck off the remaining flesh!

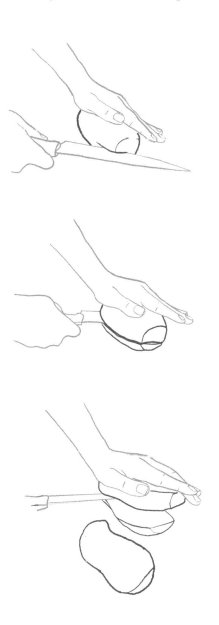

Cutting Pineapple

Cut off the top leaves (crown) and the bottom base. Stand the pineapple up on its bottom and, holding it with one hand, carefully draw your knife from top to bottom, working your way round it, cutting through the skin and peeling it off as you go. Once all the skin has been removed, run the knife down any sides that still have any brown bits left. Rinse the skinned pineapple under cold water. Then cut the pineapple in half, slice it into either spears or half-moons, and cut out the core. Slice or dice as needed.

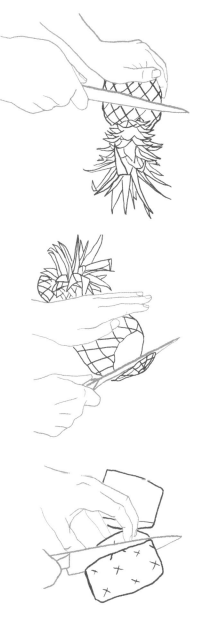

Buying Coconuts

When you're purchasing a fresh coconut, shake it and listen for the amount of water it contains, as this will indicate its maturity and freshness. If you can hear a good amount of water dancing inside, it is fresh. In addition, look for coconuts that are brown in colour and whose "three eyes" are clean with no surrounding mildew.

Notes on Jackfruit

Jackfruit is the largest tree fruit in the world, and quite astounding to see up close.

Something you may not know is that a jackfruit has several life stages—young or baby jackfruit (*polos*), mature jackfruit (*kos*), and overripe jackfruit (*waraka*)—and its flavour at each stage is different. While young jackfruit has a neutral flavour and is eaten cooked, mature and overripe jackfruit has a strong, sweet taste and is eaten raw.

The *polos* curry recipe in this book (see page 91) uses the young or baby jackfruit, also referred to as green jackfruit. Brined young green jackfruit is readily available in Asian and Indian markets in cans (not fresh).

Notes on Lentils

Like rice, lentils come in many varieties and double in volume when cooked. Wash lentils under cold water prior to cooking. For cooking, the general rule is a 1:2 ratio of lentils to water; however, in preparing dal curry recipes in this book, I begin with water to cover the lentils an inch above their surface and then add a ¼ cup at a time during cooking, as needed, to better control how much liquid is absorbed by the lentils (so as not to make them mushy) and how much liquid remains in the dish. For example, since milk is also added to the yellow dal curry recipe at the end of cooking, you want to make sure the dish does not become soupy. Cooking time of lentils also tends to be very quick (red split lentils cook in approximately 15 minutes), so you want to stay near the stove while the lentils are cooking. Lentils require quite a bit of salt for seasoning; add it when they are close to being done.

Notes on Washing Rice

Place the rice in a large enough bowl, and under a tap of cold running water, allow the water to fill until it just covers the rice. Using one hand to hold the bowl, use your free hand to wash the rice by swirling it around in the water, allowing for any dirt or particles to loosen. Tip the bowl and slowly pour out the water being careful not to let the grains spill out. (Hold the grains back with a cupped hand.) Repeat until the water runs clear.

Traditional Cooking Methods

Slow-Cooking and Enhancing the Flavour of Meats and Jackfruit

To enhance the flavour of meat curries, cover the pot soon after the meat has been added so the meat releases its natural juices (around 5 minutes). You will be surprised at how much depth of flavour this simple step adds to both the meat and the spices. The heat is then turned down to low and the curry permitted to cook slowly with a bit of coconut milk for 1 hour (or more). Similar to cooking stew, the process enriches the gravy and softens the meat.

Fibrous jackfruits should be allowed to simmer over low heat for an even longer period (at least 2 hours) so they become soft. There is a Sinhalese term used—*thel pathuma*—during the cooking process of jackfruit curry that refers specifically to the separation of the oil, which surfaces after about an hour. This is what is desired, as it indicates that you have the right flavour and consistency.

Tempering

Tempering is a common cooking method in Sri Lanka that involves the quick shallow sautéing of onions, curry leaves, and sometimes mustard seeds or ground spices. The purpose of it is to flash release the aromatics of the ingredients. Generally, oil is heated to a high temperature (but not smoking) to allow instant browning and the release of flavour. Other ingredients are added after the initial tempering.

When recipes in this book call for tempering ingredients, use the following approach:

- Place a clean pot or frying pan over high heat for a minute. Add approximately 2 tablespoons of cooking oil and allow it to reach a high heat (but again, not smoking—it's ready when slight ripples appear in it).
- Add the ingredients to the hot oil and quickly stir them to allow instant browning and the release of flavour.
- Onions are usually added to the pan first, and right as they hit the hot oil they should make a sizzling sound. They are then tempered to a golden brown; this should take 1–2 minutes. Curry leaves and *pandanus* leaves are usually added soon afterward and quickly stirred back and forth for about 15 seconds. (You don't want them to burn or overheat.) Mustard seeds are sometimes tempered separately and are kept in the hot oil until they "pop." (The individual seeds will literally make a popping sound and jump in the pan after about 30 seconds to 1 minute.)
- After tempering, continue the recipe instructions.

Other Methods

There are some dishes in this book that are not curries and whose recipes include little or no liquid, but instead involve pan-frying in oil. These dishes—for example, *Harak Mas Gam Miris Pol Kiri Badthum* (page 117), *Uru Mas Badthum* (page 121), and *Rathu Ala Badthum* (page 69)—are classified as *badthums*. After the main ingredients are cooked, sliced onion, tomatoes, and/or mild peppers are added for texture, crunch, and colour. These dishes can offer a nice contrast as part of a meal as they add a further dimension of texture. While coconut oil is the standard choice for cooking curries in Sri Lanka, olive oil, other vegetable-based oils, or grape seed oil also give good results. Just ensure you use a good-quality oil, as this makes a significant difference to the final product. And always use a large pan with enough surface area to hold the ingredients without crowding. The final dish should glisten lightly (rather than appear oily).

Texture and Consistency of Dishes

Curries

The gravy of a curry should lightly coat the main ingredient of the dish (whether it is meat, fish, fruit, or vegetable) and moisten the main grain (for example, rice, roti, or another grain). During the cooking process, if much of the coconut milk is boiled down, the curry will have a thick gravy. But the consistency of the curry can always be adjusted by adding more liquid. The consistency of a curry depends on the amount of coconut milk that is added. Different recipes call for different amounts of milk, but generally speaking, for many curries, the consistency of the liquid is similar to that of a thin sauce—there should be some substance to it, but without the thickness of a flour-based gravy. In terms of proportion, there should be slightly less liquid compared to the main ingredient. Usually vegetable curries—for example, beetroot, potato, or cauliflower—have more gravy and a thinner gravy than meat or fish curries. With starchy vegetables, such as potatoes or squash, that quickly soak up and absorb liquid (even after the dish has been removed from the heat), it is important to maintain an adequate amount of gravy to avoid a clumsy, bulky curry. (For this reason, sometimes it is helpful to boil potatoes ahead of time—that way they absorb less of the milk while cooking.) For meat and fish curries, a slightly thicker gravy is desirable because it coats the pieces nicely and keeps the meat moist.

There are also a few curries in which the main

43

ingredient (usually a vegetable) is deep-fried first, and then simmered in coconut milk and spices. This is often done with vegetables like okra and eggplant because they have a soft texture and can become mushy (and in the case of okra, slightly slimy) when cooked in coconut milk. The deep-frying absorbs the excess liquid and creates a delicious crispy outer skin that holds the pieces of vegetables together when they are later cooked in coconut milk. If you are using lentils or cashew nuts, however, some recipes may recommend soaking them before cooking to soften them and shorten the cooking time. Dal curry (*parippu*) should be soft, and the lentils completely cooked through. Milk is added to dal but be careful as you add it—you could end up with soup.

Many of the recipes in this book call for approximately 3 tablespoons to ¼ cup of coconut milk, and sometimes water may be added. Begin with the smaller volume of milk specified and gradually add more as desired. Curries are often gently simmered in a covered pot on low heat, or with the lid slightly ajar, to control evaporation.

Mallums and *Sambols*

While an ample amount of oil is a necessity for achieving the right flavour and consistency for some dishes, others use none at all. Sri Lankan *mallums* are the island's version of a leafy salad and are possibly the most nutritious complement to a meal. They are made from just about any edible green leaves, very finely cut, and then quickly dry-roasted in a pan with a little scraped coconut and just a few other ingredients. The leaves should look appetizing (not overcooked) and delicate and can be served warm. Some *mallums* are also made from unripe fruits such as papaya, mango, or even the banana flower.

Sambols are uncooked mixtures of raw fruit or vegetables where the main ingredient (usually coconut or onion) is mixed with just a few additional spices or ingredients. Coconut is finely grated and onions are either ground almost to a paste or diced. *Sambols* should appear light and fresh. Both *mallums* and *sambols* are served in small portions as side dishes.

Salads (*Sambolas*)

Salad ingredients are prepped, chopped, and/or fried and set aside and dressed just before serving. Lime juice is often a key ingredient for dressings, as is white vinegar mixed with sugar, salt, and pepper (no oil).

12   PALMS BY THE SEA, MOUNT LAVINIA, CEYLON.

RECIPES

Sri Lankan food is a reflection of the island's natural diversity, as well as its colonial past, with richly diverse culinary influences from the Portuguese, the Dutch, and the British. The Portuguese imprint on Sri Lankan cuisine can be seen in the vegetables used, such as chilies, tomatoes, and eggplants, as well as cooking methods such as tempering. The Portuguese were also known to have contributed to sweet desserts and breads in the Sri Lankan tradition. The Dutch culinary tradition in Sri Lanka may be seen in many cherished desserts such as Christmas cake or *kokis* (from the Dutch *koekje*, "cookie"), a crispy sweet made from rice flour and coconut milk, deep-fried in a wheel or flower-shaped mould. The Dutch Burgher community, which includes a mix of Portuguese, Dutch, and British, introduced the well-known and highly favoured *lamprais*: savoury small portions of richly flavoured rice, curried meats, and vegetables baked in a wrapping of banana leaves. During the British colonial period, tea cultivation in the Central Province took precedence and along with it came "tea-time." Sri Lanka's culture of afternoon tea, accompanied by small bites or hand-held desserts, is still very much intact today.

Grains

Milk Rice
Kiri Bath

This simple dish has strong cultural significance and is mostly reserved for special occasions, and in particular, for Sinhalese New Year's Day, on April 14. Served at breakfast time, it is a symbol for abundance, prosperity, harvest, and good fortune. My grandmother's milk rice was prepared in a clay pot (*muttiya*) over an open hearth with red rice and fresh coconut milk. The kernel of the coconut would be scraped and then pressed for several extracts of milk, with the first extract being the thickest and the following extracts being increasingly thinner. The rice would be cooked first with the thin milk and finished with the first press of thick milk.

In Sri Lanka, a short-grain red rice (*kakulu hal*) is typically used for the preparation of milk rice. Kakulu rice is unmilled rice. For this recipe, I suggest using jasmine rice for its naturally sticky texture and faster cooking time. Milk rice is often served with relish-style accompaniments—for example, *lunu miris sambol* (page 153), and *seeni sambol*—or with beef curry (page 115) and *pol sambol* (page 152). And if you are able to acquire them, milk rice is also often eaten simply with sweet treacle (palm tree syrup) or *jaggery* (unrefined palm tree sugar) and a side plate of baby (sugar) bananas (*seeni kesel*).

❦

Wash the rice and place it in a large pot. Start with adding 3 cups water and the salt. Place the pot of rice over medium-high heat and bring the rice, uncovered, to a boil. Turn down the heat to medium-low and let cook, covered, stirring occasionally, until the rice grains are cooked completely through. To test for doneness, try biting a grain of rice; it should not be mushy but rather firm and cooked through. Add water if needed.

Once the rice is cooked, and the water is gone, turn down the heat to low and add the coconut milk and additional salt (if needed) to the rice and stir gently with a wooden spoon to combine. Let cook until the milk is completely absorbed, about 10 minutes. The milk rice should be the consistency of thick porridge.

Pour out the milk rice in the centre of a large round or oval serving dish. It should almost fall out of the pot in one lump. Spread and smooth the rice into a round or oval (match the shape of the dish you're using) using the back of a broad spoon (or spatula), about an inch from the edge of the dish. Smooth the edges of the milk rice.

Using a sharp knife, neatly cut criss-cross lines across the rice to create a diamond pattern. Serve with suggested accompaniments.

Serves 4

2 cups jasmine rice

1½ tsp salt, or to taste

1 cup coconut milk

Use jasmine rice, which already has a sticky texture when cooked.

Fancy Yellow Rice
Kaha Bath

Yellow rice is a festive Sri Lankan dish usually served at large gatherings or on special occasions. I recall my mother serving this beautiful dish on large silver platters for the many dinner parties she hosted, and it was always a hit, with barely a grain left by the end of the night.

The rice is shaded yellow by the addition of turmeric or saffron strands, cooked with warmed ghee, and perfumed with whole cardamom pods, peppercorns, cloves, and cinnamon. It is garnished with fried hard-boiled eggs, fried cashew nuts and raisins, and a sprinkling of freshly chopped mint. It is delicious with chicken curry (page 111), white potato curry (page 65), and pineapple salad (page 147), but is flavourful enough to eat on its own. While this rice does take some time to prepare, it is well worth it. (If you want to make this for a smaller group, simply halve all the ingredients and follow the same method.)

In a small pot, melt the ghee (or butter) over medium-high heat. When the butter is hot, add the onion and fry until golden. Add 2 cups tepid water to the pot.

Add the cardamom pods, cloves, and peppercorns to the ghee and onion mixture. Cook, stirring occasionally, for 3 minutes to release and combine all the flavours.

Pour the ghee mixture into the rice cooker or the pot you are using to cook the rice. Add the washed and drained rice and the necessary amount of water required to cook the rice (see page 22). Pour the dissolved turmeric (or saffron) over the rice, insert the *pandanus* leaf into the rice, and add salt to taste. Let cook, covered.

After 15 minutes, insert the cinnamon stick directly into the rice and leave it there until ready to serve (even after the rice has finished cooking, approximately 20–25 minutes).

If you have cooked the rice in a rice cooker, keep it on the warm setting until you are ready to plate on serving dishes.

To make the garnish, in a shallow frying pan over medium-high heat, add about 2 Tbsp of oil. When the oil is hot (but not smoking), add the raisins and turn down the heat to medium. The raisins will initially balloon or swell up. Fry until lightly browned, stirring occasionally with a wooden spoon, and then remove from the pan with a slotted spoon and set onto paper towels to absorb any excess oil and let cool.

While the oil is still hot, add the cashews. Watch them carefully, as nuts cook quickly and can burn easily. Stirring gently, occasionally turn the cashews

Serves 8

RICE

¼ cup ghee or butter

½ small red onion, very finely chopped

8 cardamom pods

8 whole cloves

4–6 white peppercorns or 8–10 black peppercorns

4 cups basmati rice, washed and drained

½ tsp ground turmeric (or a few saffron strands), dissolved in 2 Tbsp of boiling water

2-inch-long piece of *pandanus* leaf, fresh or frozen

½ tsp salt

1 (2-inch) cinnamon stick

GARNISH

Olive oil

¼ cup golden or dark raisins

¼ cup cashew nuts (whole or halved)

8 small hard-boiled eggs, peeled and kept whole

1 Tbsp finely chopped fresh mint

in the pan with a spoon to ensure even browning on all sides. Fry until golden brown, about 3 minutes, and then remove from the pan with a slotted spoon and set onto paper towels to absorb any excess oil and let cool.

Before frying the hard-boiled eggs, carefully prick them all over their surface with a fork. (This will prevent them from bursting when they are placed into the hot oil.) You may want to wipe out the pan and use fresh oil for frying the eggs, as there may be pieces of nuts in the oil now. If so, use 2 Tbsp of oil again, warm it over medium-high heat, and turn down the heat to medium, once you've added the eggs. Fry the eggs one or two at a time (depending on the size of the pan). The surface of the eggs will bubble. (This is fine, as the skins will shrink down when cooled.) Gently roll the eggs around in the pan with a spoon to ensure even browning on all sides, being careful not to break them. They should be fried just until they are light golden brown in colour on all sides, about 3 minutes per egg. Remove from the pan with a slotted spoon, set on paper towels and gently pat dry (to absorb excess oil), and let cool. Once they have cooled, halve each one lengthwise.

To serve, give the rice a stir/fluff with a fork and spoon the rice out onto one large or two medium-size serving platters. Remove the *pandanus* leaf and cinnamon stick from the rice. Sprinkle the top of the rice with the fried raisins and cashew nuts. Arrange the sliced eggs (yolks facing down) in a ring on top of the rice. Finish with a sprinkling of mint.

The use of pandanus leaves is distinctive to Sri Lankan cooking, and a little bit of the leaf is used in most all curries. You need only use a small (1-inch) piece for curries, and a couple of larger (2-inch) pieces for rice dishes. It is a tough, fibrous leaf, so it is recommended that it be removed from dishes prior to serving. Fresh pandanus leaves may be cut and stored in the freezer.

Ghee Rice
Elagi Thel Bath

This aromatic ghee rice is similar to fancy yellow rice (page 53), but it includes a more generous addition of spices and is simmered in stock as the rice cooks. This rice is a nice option for rice and curries packed in banana leaves (page 61). The recipe can be halved easily.

In a small pot, melt the ghee over medium-high heat. Add the onion and fry until golden. Then add the cloves, peppercorns, lemon grass, and *pandanus* leaf and stir everything for another minute or two to release and combine the flavours.

If you are cooking the rice in a rice cooker, pour the ghee mixture into the rice cooker. (Otherwise, transfer it to the pot you are using to cook the rice on the stove.) Add the washed rice, the stock, salt, and 3½ cups of water and let cook. (Add ½ cup more water as needed.)

When the rice has been cooking for 10 minutes, stir in the cardamom pods and continue cooking the rice until it is done (another 15 minutes approximately). If you have cooked the rice in a rice cooker, keep it on the warm setting until you are ready to serve. Remove the *pandanus* leaf and lemon grass stalk before serving.

Serves 8–10

½ cup ghee

½ small red or yellow onion, chopped

10 whole cloves

20 black peppercorns

1-inch-long piece fresh lemon grass

2-inch-long piece *pandanus* leaf, fresh or frozen

4 cups long-grain white basmati rice (washed)

2 cups chicken stock

1 tsp salt

10 cardamom pods

Use a rice cooker! You can make the rice in advance of your guests arriving and leave it on the warm setting. Garnish when ready to serve on platters.

Coconut Roti
Pol Roti

At my grandmother's home in Peradeniya a breakfast of hot coconut roti and fresh coconut *sambol* was a wonderful start to the day.

In fact, these are delicious any time of day, and when served at lunch or dinner they are accompanied by coconut *sambol* and a meat curry.

Once the dough is prepared, it is rolled into balls and flattened into individual rounds, then flipped into a hot pan. Keep an eye on them as you brown each side, as you're also preparing the next roti, so you can keep things moving. As a beginner, don't worry as much about making the rounds into perfect circles as you do getting the method down as you go.

Place a square piece of parchment/wax paper on which you will mould each individual roti on your work surface. It should be just small enough to handle but large enough to work on (approximately 8 inches by 8 inches; you may wish to precut a few to have handy). Once each roti is shaped, it will be easier to take on the wax paper to the pan and then carefully drop it in.

In a large bowl, place the coconut, soft butter, and 2 cups water. Gradually add the flour, 1 cup at a time, kneading the mixture into a large ball. The mixture should be moist but not sticky. (It should not stick to the bowl or your hands. Add a little bit more flour if needed.) Let rest for 15 minutes.

Keep a bowl of cold water next to you as you prepare the roti.

Dampen your fingers and palms with water and pull off a piece of dough, slightly smaller than a tennis ball.

Dampen your hands again and flatten and shape the ball of dough into a 6-inch round on the wax paper surface.

Set a wide non-stick, ungreased, frying pan over medium-high heat. When the pan is hot, place the roti in it. Sprinkle the side that is facing up with a little water (use a tablespoon to sprinkle and smooth across the surface). When the moisture on the side facing up has evaporated, prepare to flip the roti.

Each roti will take approximately 3 minutes per side to cook. Once flipped, the cooked side facing up will be speckled with dark brown patches.

Use your spatula or the back of a spoon to firmly press across the face of the roti to let out the air and moisture (you will hear popping and squeaking sounds) and ensure the roti has cooked through.

Repeat with the remaining dough. Serve hot!

Makes approximately 12–14 roti

2½ cups fresh scraped coconut or frozen grated coconut, thawed

3 Tbsp butter, room temperature

4½ cups all-purpose flour

½ tsp fine sea salt

Use frozen coconut (see page 34) for this recipe and make the side or accompanying dishes such as coconut sambol (page 152) or beef curry (page 115) in advance.

Rice and Curries Packed in Banana Leaves
Batmula

Growing up in Canada, weekend family road trips were a good reason for my mother to prepare wonderful parcels of rice and curries wrapped in banana leaves. She would make the curries and assemble the packages either early in the morning or a day in advance and warm them just prior to our trip. We would pile into the car with our thermos of sweet milk tea and rice parcels and my father would venture out on scenic drives. Eventually, he would find a way off the main roads to a serene rest area near water to break for lunch. Sitting at the water's edge, he would carefully unfold the fragrant banana leaves of his rice parcel to open an even more aromatic bundle of rice and curries.

See page 39 for how to prepare the banana leaves and how to wrap rice and curries.

Rice bundles may be frozen for later consumption, but should be used within a week if they are wrapped in banana leaves. If you want to freeze them for longer, wrap the parcels in the same manner with the banana leaves (or alternatively parchment paper) but also wrap them in an outer layer of aluminum foil. When you remove them from the freezer, set them to thaw in the fridge. Remove the aluminum foil and reheat the thawed parcels on a baking tray in a preheated 350°F oven for 25 minutes (35–40 minutes for frozen packets). To test for doneness, open the parcel and stick a fork into the centre of the rice parcel and taste a small piece of rice.

Prepare the rice and curries in advance. For this recipe, it's good to let the rice cool a little before you use it.

Prepare the banana leaves as instructed on page 39.

Set one prepared banana leaf on top of a dinner plate in front of you. (This will help portion the serving and keep it centred as you assemble the curries.) Using a 1-cup measure (or small bowl), scoop 1 cup of rice from the pot and mould it into the shape of an upside-down bowl in the centre of the banana leaf (in the centre of the dinner plate). Then, using a tablespoon, place 2 to 3 Tbsp of each curry around the outer edges of the rice. Place one fish cutlet on the centre of the rice.

Wrap the parcels and close with a banana leaf tie (see page 39).

Pack for a picnic and enjoy!

Makes 10 packets

Prepare the following in advance. Packets are meant to be on the smaller side, with 1 cup of rice per packet, and modest servings of each of the curries:

10 cups cooked yellow rice without the fancy garnish (page 53) or ghee rice (page 57)

Fried plantain curry (page 95)

Coconut *sambol* (page 152) or raw papaya *mallum* (page 151)

Eggplant pickle (page 154)

Peppered beef with coconut milk and mustard seeds (page 117)

10 fried fish cutlets (page 161)

Banana leaves, enough for 10 packets

Vegetable Dishes

White Potato Curry
Suthu Ālā Curry

If you like simple, creamy flavours, you will love this white curry recipe. It is a staple hill country dish, one that my grandmother often served on the lunch table and one that my mother often made at home. This beautiful yet uncomplicated dish is easy to prepare. This curry's colour is a brilliant yellow due to the turmeric. Since it is mild in flavour, it is a great dish for both young and old. It goes nicely with brown or red rice, parsley salad (page 145), and jackfruit curry (page 91). (This recipe doubles easily.)

Traditionally this curry is made with small white potatoes, sliced into evenly sized quarters. You can also use baby or red potatoes.

Choose a waxy potato variety that has a low to medium-low starch content. Mealy varieties like russet do not work well for curries because they have a higher starch content and become fluffy and dry, almost crumbly, when cooked.

Cut the baby potatoes in half or if you use larger potatoes, quarter them (and halve the quarters if they are large).

Put the potatoes, onion, turmeric, fenugreek seeds, chili, curry leaves, *pandanus* leaf, and salt in a pot, and add enough water (approximately 1–1½ cups) to just cover the potatoes. Cook, covered, over medium-high heat for approximately 15 minutes.

Add ¼ cup of the coconut milk and more salt if desired, and gently stir to combine the flavours. Turn down the heat to its lowest setting and let simmer, covered, for approximately 5 to 10 minutes.

Finish by squeezing the lime wedge over the curry. Stir, remove from the heat, and let stand for 5 to 10 minutes.

Serves 4

1 lb small white or baby potatoes, peeled

¼ small red onion, chopped

½ tsp ground turmeric

¼ tsp fenugreek seeds

1 whole green (Thai) chili (optional)

3–4 curry leaves, ripped into small pieces

1 inch-long piece of *pandanus* leaf

1 tsp fine sea salt, or to taste

¼–½ cup coconut milk (or full-fat cow's milk)

1 small lime wedge (yielding about 1 tsp juice)

Red Potato Curry
Ǟla Maluwa

Potatoes have long been a part of the regional diet in Sri Lanka's Central Highlands. Just as they come in many varieties, so too are there many ways to prepare them. In this red curry recipe the optional addition of dried Maldives fish brings a distinctive coastal flavour to the dish. Serve with coconut roti (page 59) and coconut *sambol* (page 152).

Cut the parboiled potatoes into cubes.

In a bowl, place half the chopped red onions, the cayenne, paprika, curry powder, turmeric, fenugreek seeds, curry leaves, Maldives fish (if using), salt to taste, coconut milk, and ¼ cup water. Squeeze the lime wedge over top. Mix to combine.

In a frying pan over high heat, warm the olive oil. When the oil is hot, add the remaining chopped red onion and temper (see page 42) until golden, then add the mustard seeds. When the mustard seeds begin to pop, add the coconut milk mixture to the pan. Bring to a boil, add the potatoes, turn the heat down to low, and simmer, uncovered, for 10 minutes.

Remove from the heat and let sit for a few minutes before serving.

Serves 4

1 lb white or red potatoes, parboiled and peeled

½ small red onion, finely chopped, and divided

½ tsp cayenne powder

½ tsp paprika

½ tsp roasted curry powder (page 31)

¼ tsp ground turmeric

Pinch of fenugreek seeds

5 curry leaves, ripped into small pieces

½ tsp dried Maldives fish (optional)

1 tsp fine sea salt, or to taste

½ cup coconut milk

1 small lime wedge (yielding about 1 tsp juice)

2 Tbsp olive oil

1 tsp black mustard seeds

Devilled Potatoes
Ala Badthum

Devilled potato melds savoury, fiery, and spicy flavours. The colourful spices give the humble potato a wonderful makeover, but it still has a warm, soft texture on the inside and a subtly crispy coating on the outside. Serve with yellow rice without the garnish (page 53), fried fish cutlets (page 161), kale *mallum* (page 150), and cucumber salad (page 135).

❧

Boiling the potatoes in advance ensures a soft texture on the inside after they are added to the pan for shallow-frying.

I use baby potatoes for this dish as they are easy to cut into halves which make small, evenly sized pieces, and they cook relatively quickly, but small white waxy potatoes work as well.

Cut the cooked potatoes into halves. (If you use small white potatoes, cut them into cubes.) Place them in a bowl and add the paprika, turmeric, cayenne, chili flakes, and salt. Squeeze the lime wedge over top, and mix all the ingredients together with a wooden spoon.

Heat 1 Tbsp of the oil with the butter (or ghee, if using) in a frying pan over medium-high heat. When the oil is hot and the butter melted, add the onion and fry until translucent and starting to brown, and then add the curry leaves. Stir to combine and release flavours for 1 to 2 minutes.

Add the potato mixture to the pan, stirring the ingredients to combine and being careful not to break the potatoes. You may have to add another 1 Tbsp oil and salt to taste.

Turn down the heat to medium-low and let crisp, 10 to 15 minutes. Occasionally lift the pan off the heat and toss the potatoes so they crisp on all sides.

Serves 4

- 1 lb baby white potatoes, boiled and peeled
- 1 tsp paprika
- ¼ tsp ground turmeric
- ¼ tsp cayenne powder
- ¼–½ tsp crushed chili flakes (according to taste)
- ½ tsp fine sea salt, or to taste
- 1 small lime wedge (yielding about 1 tsp juice)
- 2 Tbsp olive oil, divided
- 1 Tbsp butter or ghee (optional)
- ½ small red onion, coarsely chopped
- 8–10 curry leaves, ripped into small pieces

Fried Beetroots
Rathu Ala Badthum

Beetroot is one of my favourite vegetables for its versatility, rustic quality, and sweet flavour. This vegetable adds colour, substance, and nutrition to a meal, and tastes wonderful in a variety of curries and dishes. This particular recipe has a sweet, savoury, and peppery taste with a bit of sour. It pairs well with sour fish curry (page 129) or chicken curry (page 111), mung bean curry (page 104), and a kale *mallum* (page 150).

❧

If banana peppers are not available or in season, an Anaheim or a Cubanelle pepper is a good substitute.

Peel the beets, trim the stems and tips, and thinly slice off any dark patches. Cut them into thick wedges and place the pieces in a bowl. Add the vinegar, salt, and pepper, and mix to combine.

In a wide frying pan, melt the butter in the oil over high heat. When the oil is hot, add the onion and curry leaves for 1 to 2 minutes. Stir to release flavours for a couple of minutes.

Add the beet mixture to the pan, stir to combine, cover, and turn the heat down to low for 5 minutes. Add the banana pepper, stir to combine, and let fry uncovered for another few minutes. Squeeze the lime over the beets and mix in the juice.

Remove from the heat and let stand for a few minutes before serving.

Serves 4–6

1 lb small red beetroots, boiled and cooled

2 Tbsp white vinegar

1 tsp fine sea salt, or to taste

½ tsp ground black pepper

1 Tbsp butter or ghee

1 Tbsp olive oil

½ cup yellow onion, cut in thick slices

10 curry leaves, ripped into small pieces

1 banana pepper, thickly sliced on the diagonal

1 small lime wedge (yielding about 1 tsp juice)

Try using either canned whole beets or ready-to-eat (cooked, peeled) packaged whole baby beets. These come in varying weights so only use what you need for this recipe. If I'm boiling raw beets, I often make a few extra for later use in salads or ribbon sandwiches (page 163).

Beetroot Curry
Rathu Ala Maluwa

This curry kindles childhood memories, as I absolutely adored beetroot curry as a young girl—hard to believe because what kid eats their vegetables and, of all things, beetroot? Well, for a little girl, the kind of vegetable that turns your white rice pink is perfect! This truly is an opportunity to play with your food, and the delicious, mildly sweet, creamy flavour of this curry doesn't hurt either. This curry is not only pleasing for children; parents will appreciate its highly nutritious qualities and relatively quick cooking time. This hill country curry is healthy, filling, and a lovely complement to a meal of white short- or long-grain rice, jackfruit curry (page 91), and kale *mallum* (page 150).

Peel the beetroots and trim the stems and tips. Cut the beetroots into ¼-inch thick slices and then cut the slices evenly into matchsticks about 1½ inches long.

Place the beetroots, chili, onion, salt, and fenugreek seeds in a pot. Add enough water to just cover the beetroots (approximately 1 cup) and bring to a boil, uncovered, over medium-high heat. Turn down the heat to low and let cook, partly covered, until the beets are fork-tender, approximately 15 minutes.

Pour the coconut milk into the pot and add more salt if desired. Lift the pot and move it in a circular, swirling motion to mix the milk into the curry. Return to the heat and let simmer for a few minutes. Finish by squeezing the lime wedge over top, swirling to combine the flavours again.

Let sit for a few minutes to allow the flavours to blend before serving.

Serves 4–6

1 lb small red beetroots

1 whole green (Thai) chili (optional)

¼ small red onion, finely chopped

½ tsp fine sea salt, or to taste

¼ tsp fenugreek seeds

½ cup coconut milk (or full-fat cow's milk)

1 small lime wedge (yielding about 1 tsp juice)

Winter Squash Curry
Wattakka Curry

In North America, winter squash, yams, and pumpkins are associated with the warmth of fall harvests. We tend to think of them as being prepared as sweet and spicy fillings for pies and tarts, or as tasty side dishes that have been oven-roasted with sprinklings of brown sugar and herbs. In Sri Lanka, pumpkin curry has all the qualities you would expect of comfort food. Because it is filling you can eat less rice with it. Enjoy this dish with coconut *sambol* (page 152) or papaya *mallum* (page 151) and a simple white fish curry (page 127).

Kabocha, buttercup, and acorn squash all work well for this recipe.

In Sri Lanka, the local varieties of pumpkin (similar to kabocha) typically used in curry have yellow flesh and are cooked with their green edible skin left on.

Cut the squash in half. Discard the seeds and pulp and cut the flesh into even 2-inch small wedges or cubes.

In a medium pot over medium-high heat, place the squash, onion, garlic, chili, curry leaves, fenugreek, turmeric, salt to taste, and about ½ cup of water. Bring to a boil, cover, and let cook over medium heat until squash is tender but not mushy, approximately 10 minutes.

In the meantime, using a mortar and pestle, finely grind the mustard seeds. Place 1 tsp of the ground mustard seeds in a small bowl, add the coconut milk, and stir to combine.

Check the squash and add more water, ¼ cup at a time, only if necessary.

Add the coconut milk mixture and more salt, if preferred, to the pot. Lift the pot from the heat and move it in a circular swirling motion to mix the coconut milk into the curry. Turn down the heat to its lowest setting and let simmer, partially covered, for approximately 5 minutes to meld the flavours.

Squeeze the lime wedge over top. Remove the pot from the heat and swirl it again to combine all the flavours. Let sit for a few minutes before serving.

Serves 4–6

- 1 lb kabocha squash, washed but unpeeled
- ¼ red onion, chopped
- 1 garlic clove, smashed
- 1 green (Thai) chili, cut in half on the diagonal
- 4–6 curry leaves, ripped into small pieces
- ¼ tsp fenugreek seeds
- ¼ tsp ground turmeric
- ½ tsp fine sea salt, or to taste
- 1 tsp yellow or black mustard seeds
- ½ cup coconut milk
- 1 small lime wedge (yielding about 1 tsp juice)

If your grocery store has a produce clerk, ask them to cut the squash in half for you. This will make it easier for you to core and chop once you get home. Save the unused portion for soup!

Carrot Curry
Carrot Maluwa

This recipe may not reflect what most North Americans expect of a South Asian curry or tropical dish, but root vegetables are plentiful in Sri Lanka's hill country. The earthy sweetness of carrots mixed with coconut milk and distinctive mustard seeds creates an exotic yet rural dish. This curry pairs well with white rice, cashew nut curry (page 99), and eggplant salad (page 143).

Cut the carrots into thick, short sticks (about 2 inches long and 1 inch wide).

Place the carrots, green chili, onions, curry powder, paprika, cayenne, turmeric, and salt to taste in a large pot. Add just enough cold water to cover.

Bring to a boil, uncovered, over high heat. Once the water is boiling, turn the heat down to low, cover, and simmer until the carrots are cooked. Add the coconut milk and more salt, if preferred. Using the handle of the pot, lift the pot off the heat and move it in a circular swirling motion to mix the coconut milk into the curry. Let simmer on the lowest heat, uncovered, while you proceed with the next step.

In a frying pan over high heat, place oil. When it's hot, add the mustard seeds. When the seeds start popping (less than a minute), add the carrot curry directly to the pan, turn the heat down to low, and partially cover to shield you and your kitchen from the splatter. Remove the lid when the curry is at a simmer and let cook for another 3–5 minutes.

Remove from the heat and let stand for 5 minutes before serving.

Serves 4–6

1 lb large carrots

1 green (Thai) chili, cut in half on the diagonal

¼ small red or yellow onion, chopped

½ tsp roasted curry powder (page 31)

¼ tsp paprika

¼ tsp cayenne pepper

¼ tsp ground turmeric

½ tsp fine sea salt, or to taste

¼ cup coconut milk (or full-fat cow's milk)

1 Tbsp olive oil

½ tsp black mustard seeds

Tempered Leeks
Leeks Thel Dala

When driving through Nuwara Eliya as a child, I would be in awe of the abundance of potatoes, beets, and leeks being sold by local farmers along the roadsides. Today, Nuwara Eliya produces the vast majority of leeks in the country, cultivated throughout the year. This dish is a common side accompaniment to meals. Because leeks have a mild onion flavour that doesn't overpower other flavours, it pairs well with white or brown rice, beef curry (page 115), carrot slaw (page 138), and devilled potatoes (page 67).

Cut off the dark green tops of the leeks and trim the roots, preserving some of the edible light-green leaves and the whole white portion and bulb. Slit the white bulb lengthwise and thoroughly wash out any dirt. Thinly slice the leeks into half-moons approximately ¼ to ⅓-inch wide, and place in a bowl. Add the turmeric and salt to taste, and stir to combine.

Set a wide frying pan over high heat and add oil. When the oil is hot, add the curry leaves, garlic, and chili flakes and temper (see page 42) for 1 to 2 minutes, to release the aromatics and flavours.

Add the leeks to the pan and temper, stirring them back and forth quickly over medium-high heat, until tender but not mushy, 5 to 8 minutes. Add salt to taste.

Serves 4–6

1 lb large leeks

½ tsp ground turmeric

½ tsp fine sea salt, or to taste

2-3 Tbsp olive oil

4 curry leaves, ripped into small pieces

1 garlic clove, thinly sliced

2 tsp chili flakes

Cabbage Curry
Gova Maluwa

In Sri Lankan cooking, cabbage may be prepared a variety of ways, including tempering it with spices and oil or cooking it in a stew. This cabbage curry brings a bit of warmth on chilly days. Try it with rice and peppered beef with coconut milk and mustard seed (page 117), or string hoppers, boiled eggs with coconut milk (page 113), and coconut *sambol* (page 152).

Discard the fibrous thick stem and core of the cabbage. Chop the leaves into ½-inch pieces.

Put the cabbage, onion, chili, turmeric, fenugreek, and salt to taste in a pot and add ¼ cup water. Cook, covered, over medium-high heat until the cabbage is fork-tender, approximately 10 minutes.

In the meantime, using a mortar and pestle, finely grind the mustard seeds. Place the ground mustard seeds in a small bowl, add the coconut milk, and stir to combine.

Add the coconut milk mixture to the cabbage, with more salt if preferred, and stir to combine the flavours. Turn off the heat but leave the pot on the stovetop for a few minutes before serving.

Serves 4–6

1 lb (or ½ medium-size) white or green cabbage

¼ small red onion, chopped

1 small whole green (Thai) chili

½ tsp ground turmeric

½ tsp fenugreek seeds

1 tsp fine sea salt, or to taste

1 tsp black mustard seeds

¼ cup coconut milk

Cauliflower, Potatoes, and Green Peas Curry
Malgova, Ala, Peas Ata Maluwa

Once I asked my mother about the availability of cauliflower in Sri Lanka because it seemed unusual to me that it should grow so freely in the tropics. She was almost dismayed by my question and explained that her father grew an abundance of fresh cauliflower in the family's vegetable garden while he was the agricultural curator for the King's Pavilion in Kandy. I can only imagine how delicious every meal must have tasted, not only because the food was fresh, but also because the vegetables were nurtured by my grandfather's hands.

This curry is a nice option for larger dinner parties because the mild flavour balances well with a variety of dishes and curries. For a colourful spread, serve it with fancy yellow rice (page 53), chicken curry (page 111), beetroot curry (page 71), and fried fish cutlets (page 161).

This dish may take some practice to achieve the right consistency, so you may wish to begin with ¾ of a cup of the coconut milk and add a ¼ cup more toward the end of cooking.

Serves 4–6

- 1 lb (about half a head) white cauliflower, cored
- ½ lb white or red potatoes
- ½ cup red onion, finely chopped
- 1 small whole green (Thai) chili
- 4–6 curry leaves, ripped into small pieces
- 1-inch-long piece of *pandanus* leaf, fresh or frozen
- Heaping ¼ tsp ground turmeric
- ¼ tsp fenugreek seeds
- 1 tsp fine sea salt, or to taste
- ¾–1 cup coconut milk
- ¼ cup frozen peas
- 1 small lime wedge (yielding about 1 tsp juice)

Cut the cauliflower into bite-sized pieces and set aside.

Peel the potatoes, cut them into 1½-inch cubes.

In a large pot over medium-high heat, place the potatoes, onion, chili, curry leaves, *pandanus* leaf, turmeric, fenugreek, salt, and ¾ cup of the coconut milk. Let cook, covered, until the potatoes are parboiled, 5 to 7 minutes.

Add the cauliflower, turn down the heat to medium-low, and cover again. Let simmer, stirring occasionally, until the cauliflower is tender, approximately 15 minutes.

Add the remaining ¼ cup of coconut milk, if needed, and/or ¼ cup water, if you wish to thin the gravy slightly. Add salt to taste, and add the peas, and let cook, uncovered, for 2 minutes.

Squeeze the lime over the curry, stir to combine flavours, and remove the pot from the heat. Let sit, partially covered, for 10 to 15 minutes to blend the flavours. Remove the *pandanus* leaf before serving.

Eggplant Curry
Wambatu (Badthala) Curry

This signature Sri Lankan eggplant dish offers a complex mix of spicy, sour, salty, and sweet in a single bite. It has quite a depth of texture and flavours, so it is best served with dishes that balance and complement its vibrant and bold personality—for example, a cucumber salad (page 135), fancy yellow rice (page 53), and fried pork with onions and banana peppers (page 121).

❦

This recipe involves deep-frying. If you are using a pot to deep fry the eggplant, you may need more or less oil than specified.

You can test if the oil is ready by dropping a single piece of eggplant or a small piece of bread into it. If the oil immediately bubbles up, it is hot enough.

Cut the eggplant into evenly sized rectangular pieces, approximately 1½ inches long and ½ inch wide.

Half-fill a medium-size pot with the oil. (You may not need all 4 cups.) Heat the oil on high until it is very hot but not smoking (350° to 375°F). Fry the eggplant in small batches, taking care not to overcrowd the pot, and gently turn the pieces so they are evenly browned, until the flesh is golden brown, approximately 1 minute. Because the flesh is delicate, you have to keep a careful watch so they don't burn.

Using a slotted spoon, remove the eggplant from the pot and set the pieces on a plate that has been covered with paper towels. Using another paper towel, gently pat the pieces to remove any excess oil. Set aside.

In a bowl, mix the garlic, ginger, mustard, salt, and cayenne with the coconut milk and vinegar.

Place about 1 to 2 Tbsp of oil in a medium-size frying pan over high heat. Add all the chilies and onion and stir for about 30 seconds until the onion is golden brown, and you can smell the flavours being released. Add the coconut milk mixture, stirring frequently to combine the flavours. Bring to a boil.

Add the deep-fried eggplant to the pan and turn the heat down to low. Stir gently but frequently, being careful not to mash the pieces. Stir in the sugar. Simmer for 10 minutes (the curry will be thick with almost no gravy), then remove from the heat and serve.

Serves 4–6

1 lb long Japanese or Chinese eggplant, stem removed

Approximately 4 cups vegetable oil for frying + 1–2 Tbsp oil, divided

2 garlic cloves, finely grated or ground in a mortar and pestle

1–1½-inch piece fresh ginger, finely grated

2 Tbsp grainy mustard

½–1 tsp fine sea salt, or to taste

¼ tsp cayenne powder

½ cup coconut milk

¼ cup white vinegar

6 small red bird's eye chilies (4 thinly sliced and 2 left whole)

¼ small red onion, chopped, or ¼ cup shallots, peeled and chopped

1 Tbsp granulated sugar

Place cut eggplant in a bowl, sprinkle liberally with salt, pour 2 Tbsp oil over top, and lightly toss. Place in a layer on a greased baking sheet and bake in a 400°F oven until golden brown, approximately 20 minutes.

Okra Curry
Bandakka (Badthala) Curry

If you have had the experience of cooking with okra, also referred to as ladies' fingers, you know that its naturally slimy texture comes with the territory. My mother loves okra and prepares it a few ways, but this recipe is my favourite. The best news? The deep-frying removes all hints of sliminess! Enjoy this with jasmine rice, beef curry (page 115), parsley salad (page 145), and yellow dal (page 101).

Wash the okra, trim the tops and tails, and chop the okra on the diagonal into approximately 1-inch pieces. Pat the pieces dry.

Half-fill a medium-size pot with the oil. (You may not need all 4 cups.) Heat the oil on high until it is very hot but not smoking, 350°–375°F. Fry the okra in small batches, taking care not to overcrowd the pot and gently turning the pieces so they are evenly fried, until the skins are dull green in colour, the ridges are brown, and the interior flesh is golden brown, approximately 2 minutes. Watch the okra carefully so that the pieces do not burn or over fry.

Using a slotted spoon, remove the fried okra pieces from the pot and set them on a plate that has been covered with paper towels. Using another paper towel, gently pat the pieces to remove excess oil.

Place the pieces in a bowl and squeeze the lime wedge over top.

In a separate bowl, place half the chopped onions, the chili, curry leaves, paprika, cayenne, fenugreek, turmeric, and salt to taste. Add the coconut milk and mix to combine.

In a pot over high heat, place 2 Tbsp of oil. Add the remaining onions and lightly brown.

Add the coconut milk mixture to the browned onions. Bring to a boil, and then add the fried okra. Stir to combine.

Turn off the heat, cover, and let sit for 5 minutes before serving.

Serves 4–6

½ lb okra

Approximately 4 cups vegetable oil + 2 Tbsp oil, divided

1 small lime wedge (yielding about 1 tsp juice)

½ small red onion, chopped, divided

1 small green (Thai) chili, cut in half on the diagonal

4 curry leaves, ripped into small pieces

¼ tsp paprika

¼ tsp cayenne powder

¼ tsp fenugreek seeds

Pinch of ground turmeric

½ tsp fine sea salt, or to taste

½ cup coconut milk

Green Bean White Curry
Bonchi Suthu Curry

In Sri Lanka, climbing or runner beans are called *bonchi* in Sinhala. The tender pods are cut into thin strips or small pieces and either tempered in oil with spices or prepared with a bit of coconut milk as a curry. This is a simple, almost overlooked side dish, but is very tasty and a nice accompaniment to ghee rice (page 57), chicken curry (page 111), fried beetroot, and tomato, cucumber, and red onion salad (page 137).

Most of the vegetable curries in this book benefit from sitting for a few minutes, but before serving I recommend giving them a quick stir to combine any ingredients that may have settled on the bottom of the dish.

Cut the tips and tails from the beans, remove the strings, and halve the beans, slicing them on the diagonal.

Put the beans, onion, chilies, curry leaves, turmeric, and salt to taste in a pot with 1 cup water (just enough to cook the beans). Cover, bring to a boil, turn down the heat to medium, and continue cooking. When the beans are cooked (firm yet cooked through), add the coconut milk and more salt, if desired, and stir to ensure ingredients are mixed. Squeeze the lime wedge over top and stir to combine. Remove from the heat until ready to serve.

Serves 4–6

- 1 lb green string beans
- ¼ small red onion, sliced
- 3 small green chilies, thinly sliced on the diagonal (optional)
- 4 curry leaves, ripped into small pieces
- ¼ tsp ground turmeric
- ½ tsp fine sea salt, or to taste
- ¼ cup coconut milk
- 1 small lime wedge (yielding about 1 tsp juice)

Use frozen precut French green beans, if fresh beans are not available.

Tempered Snake Beans
Makaral Thel Dala

In Sri Lanka, there are many varieties of climbing beans, such as winged beans and snake beans. They are nutritious and easy to prepare. Snake beans, also called yard-long beans or Chinese long beans, are very long and slender, with a slightly tougher outer layer. In Sri Lankan cooking they are snapped into shorter pieces and cooked like regular green beans. This spicy dish is tasty with white rice, white potato curry (page 65), and some crunchy pappadums.

Snake beans can be found in Asian and Indian markets. If you can't find them, use the same weight of regular or French green beans and cut them as described in the recipe.

Wash the beans and cut them into 1-inch-long pieces.

Place the beans in a bowl. Add the cayenne, paprika, fenugreek, unroasted curry powder, turmeric, Maldives fish (if using), and salt to taste, and mix well. Set aside.

In a shallow frying pan, heat the oil. When the oil is hot, add the onion and curry leaves to temper (see page 42).

Add the bean mixture and stir to combine.

Add ¼ cup of water, cover, and let cook over medium-low heat until the beans are cooked but still firm to the bite, 3 to 5 minutes. Stir, and turn off the heat but let sit uncovered for another 3 to 5 minutes before serving.

Serves 4–6

½ lb snake beans (see note)

¾ tsp cayenne powder

½ tsp paprika

½ tsp fenugreek seeds

¼ tsp unroasted curry powder (page 31)

Pinch of ground turmeric

½ tsp Maldives fish (optional)

½ tsp fine sea salt, or to taste

2 Tbsp vegetable oil

¼ small red onion, finely sliced

6 curry leaves, ripped into small pieces

Fruit, Nut, and Lentil Dishes

Young Jackfruit Curry
Polos Ambula

I recall as a child being driven around the Kandy hillsides and seeing groups of jackfruits lazily hanging from the sides of trees. These enormous oval-shaped fruits with their green stubbly skins looked as though they were right out of a storybook, intending to be served like grapes to men the size of Goliath!

This dish is full of earthy, spicy, peppery flavours that are absorbed by the tender jackfruit. Each bite is succulent and nourishing. This curry is perfect for large gatherings and is nice with beetroot curry (page 71) and parsley salad (page 145).

Canned young jackfruit are usually precut into pieces that are triangular in shape, which might come as a surprise if you've never used jackfruit before.

Thel pathuma is a Sinhalese term used for the cooking process in this recipe. This refers to the separation of the oil about an hour into the cooking process, which indicates you've achieved the right consistency for this curry.

Pour the jackfruit into a sieve to drain off the excess liquid from the cans and rinse under cold running water. Cut the nose (the tip) off each triangular piece. (This is the core of the fruit.) Cut larger pieces in two. (The individual pieces should be approximately 1½ inches long and 1 inch wide.) Transfer them to a bowl and set aside.

In a large, wide pot (preferably with two handles) place the onion, *pandanus* leaf, curry leaves, brined *goraka*, cloves, cardamom pods, curry powder, paprika, cayenne, salt, turmeric, and coconut milk. Bring to a boil, uncovered, over high heat.

Once it's boiling, add the jackfruit pieces. Adjust them so they overlap as little as possible and the coconut milk is covering most of them. Turn down the heat to medium-low, cover, and let cook. Check periodically, shaking the pot gently, using the handles, to mix the flavours. Add more salt to taste.

About 1 hour into the cooking time, you should see the separation of oil that will rise to the surface. Check to see if the curry needs more liquid. If so, add ¼ cup of water. Let simmer for another hour on low heat, then turn off the heat and let sit on the stovetop for 20 minutes before serving.

Serves 6

1 lb (two 20-oz cans) young green jackfruit in brine

½ small red onion, chopped

2-inch-wide piece *pandanus* leaf, fresh or frozen

6–8 curry leaves, ripped into small pieces

4–6 segments of brined *goraka* pieces (see page 38), drained

5 whole cloves

3 green cardamom pods

3 heaping tsp roasted curry powder (page 31)

2 tsp paprika

1 tsp cayenne powder

1 tsp fine sea salt, or to taste

½ tsp ground turmeric

3 cups coconut milk

Pineapple Curry
Annasi Maluwa

Fruits like pineapple and mango are wonderful in vegetarian dishes as they have substantial texture. They stand up to the heat of cooking, absorb and enhance the flavour of the spices, and mix well with the bright aroma of curry leaves and the nutty vanilla profile of *pandanus* leaves. With the added heat of the cayenne pepper and the sharpness of the black mustard seeds, this curry will warm your tummy and leave a tingle on your tongue! This is lovely with white jasmine rice, devilled potatoes (page 67), prawn curry (page 126), and bitter gourd salad (page 141).

The fresh pineapple in this recipe cannot be substituted with canned.

Cut the pineapple into bite-size chunks (see page 41). Place them in a medium-size pot with the onion, curry leaves, chili, salt, paprika, cayenne, turmeric, and fenugreek, followed by ½ cup of water.

Cook, covered, over medium heat for 15 minutes, stirring occasionally.

Add the coconut milk, turn the heat down to low, and let simmer for approximately 10 minutes, stirring occasionally. Adjust the salt to taste.

Transfer the pineapple and the coconut milk sauce to a separate bowl or dish.

Now do your tempering. In the same pot (no need to wipe it out first) over high heat, warm the oil and temper (see page 42) the onion until golden brown. Add the curry leaves and mustard seeds to temper.

When you hear the mustard seeds start popping, quickly add the pineapple and sauce and cover the pot. Turn down the heat to its lowest setting, and simmer for approximately 10 minutes to blend the flavours. Turn off the heat and let stand for 5 minutes before serving.

Serves 4–6

1 fresh ripe pineapple (approximately 1 lb after coring, skinning, and cutting)

¼ small red onion

6 curry leaves, ripped into small pieces, divided

1 small green (Thai) chili, diced

1 tsp fine sea salt

1 tsp paprika

½ tsp cayenne powder

Pinch of ground turmeric

Pinch of fenugreek seeds

½ cup coconut milk

1½ Tbsp olive oil

2 Tbsp diced onion

4–5 curry leaves

1 tsp black mustard seeds

Fried Plantain Curry
Alu Kesel Gedi Badthum

If you travel in Sri Lanka, you are certain to see a lot of bananas. They have long been incorporated into Sri Lankan culture, festivities, and cuisine, and come in many varieties.

This recipe is perfect for rice and curries packed in banana leaves (page 61).

*In Sri Lanka, ash plantains (*alu kesel*) are the variety of banana commonly used for cooking and for this recipe. Green plantains are commonly available in Asian stores and in some grocery stores.*

Pour 1 cup of cold water into a medium bowl, mix in a pinch of salt, a pinch of turmeric, and the juice from one of the lime wedges, and set aside.

Peel the plantains and then slice them diagonally into ¼-inch-thick slices. Drop the plantain pieces into the water and swirl the bowl to rinse them. Drain off the water and pat dry the plantain pieces. Place them in a clean bowl, sprinkle the ½ tsp salt over top, and stir to combine.

Half-fill a medium-size pot with the oil. (You may not need all 4 cups.) Heat the oil on high until it is very hot but not smoking (350°–375°F). Fry the plantains in small batches, taking care not to overcrowd the pot and gently turning the pieces, until the flesh is golden brown, approximately 1 minute.

Using a slotted spoon, remove the plantain pieces from the pot and set them on a plate that has been covered with paper towels. Using another paper towel, gently pat the pieces to remove any excess oil. Set them aside.

In a bowl, mix together the coconut milk with the curry leaves, *pandanus* leaf (if using), the ¼ tsp turmeric, cayenne, curry powder, fenugreek, and the ½ tsp salt or to taste.

In a large frying pan over high heat, place the 2 Tbsp of oil. When the oil is hot, add the onion and green chilies to temper (see page 42). Add the coconut milk mixture to the pan and bring to a boil.

Add the deep-fried plantains, stir to combine, adjust the salt to taste, and then squeeze the remaining lime wedge over top.

Turn off the heat and remove the pan from the element. Let sit for 15 minutes. The plantains will completely absorb the coconut gravy.

Serves 4–6

½ tsp fine sea salt + an extra pinch, divided

¼ tsp ground turmeric + an extra pinch, divided

2 small lime wedges (yielding about 2 tsp juice)

3 green plantains

4 cups vegetable oil

½ cup coconut milk

4–6 curry leaves, ripped into small pieces

1-inch-long piece of *pandanus* leaf, fresh or frozen (optional)

1 tsp cayenne powder

¼ tsp unroasted curry powder (page 31)

¼ tsp fenugreek seeds

2 Tbsp vegetable oil

½ cup red onion, chopped

2 small (Thai) green chilies

Mango Curry
Ǣmu Ǣmba Curry

Having grown up in Colombo, my husband certainly had his fill of fresh mango from the many trees in his family's garden. A plate of sliced mango is still his favourite dessert, and even I can't resist the succulence of fresh mango. Its sweet and mildly sour flavour is addictive. This mango curry is a classic Sri Lankan dish, although I admit it's a bit of an acquired taste if you've not grown up with it. Enjoy this with plain white basmati rice.

Green mangoes are available in Asian and Indian markets. There's some deliberation over whether mangoes should be peeled or not for this curry. It is also common to include the seed in the curry. That's your decision!

Peel the mangoes if preferred, cut the cheeks on a slight angle into slices 3–4 inches long and 1 inch wide (see page 41), and place in a bowl.

Add the sugar and 1 tsp salt, mix to combine, and set aside.

In another bowl, mix the coconut milk with ½ cup water. Add the curry powder, paprika, cayenne, fenugreek, turmeric, and ½ tsp salt or to taste, mix together, and set aside.

In a large pot over high heat, place oil. When the oil is hot, add the onions. When the onion is translucent, add the mustard seeds and half the curry leaves to temper (see page 42).

When the mustard seeds start to pop and the onion is browned, add the coconut milk mixture, mangoes, remaining curry leaves, and *pandanus* leaf. Cover and let cook on medium-low until the mango pieces are tender but not mushy, approximately 10 minutes. Adjust the salt as needed. Remove from the heat and serve immediately.

Serves 4–6

- 1–1¼ lb green mangoes
- 2 tsp granulated sugar
- 1 ½ tsp fine sea salt, divided
- 1¼ cups coconut milk
- 1 tsp roasted curry powder (page 31)
- 1 tsp paprika
- ½ tsp cayenne powder
- ¼ tsp fenugreek seeds
- Pinch of ground turmeric
- 2 Tbsp olive oil
- ¼ small red onion, chopped
- 1 tsp black mustard seeds
- 6–8 curry leaves, ripped into small pieces, divided
- 1-inch-long piece of *pandanus* leaf, fresh or frozen

Tomato Curry
Thakkali Maluwa

My mother grew up eating tomatoes in Sri Lanka, just as she ate any other fruit: fresh and simply rinsed. I have always credited her beautiful skin to her healthy appetite for tomatoes. Tomatoes are a popular ingredient in Sri Lankan cuisine and are used as a thickening and tenderizing agent in curries, for a bit of added colour and texture in *sambolas*, and as a refreshing bite in salads. Serve this tomato curry with coconut roti (page 59) or string hoppers, boiled eggs with coconut milk (page 113), and coconut *sambol* (page 152).

Choose firm red tomatoes such as vine, Roma or medium-size beefsteak tomatoes.

Wash the tomatoes and slice them into wedges. Place them in a bowl and mix in the sugar and ½ tsp salt or to taste. Set aside.

In another bowl, mix the coconut milk with the garlic, cloves, cardamom pods, curry powder, cayenne, paprika, turmeric, and ½ tsp salt or to taste. Set aside.

In a frying pan over high heat, place oil. When the oil is hot, add the onion. When the onion is golden, add the curry leaves to temper (see page 42).

When the curry leaves are lightly browned, mix in the coconut milk mixture and bring to a boil.

Add the tomatoes, turn the heat down to low, and simmer, uncovered, for 15 minutes.

Serves 4–6

- 1 lb ripe, firm Roma or beefsteak tomatoes
- ¼ tsp granulated sugar
- 1 tsp fine sea salt, divided
- 1½ cups coconut milk
- 1 garlic clove, crushed
- 2 cloves
- 2 cardamom pods
- 1 tsp roasted curry powder (page 31)
- ½ tsp cayenne powder
- ½ tsp paprika
- ¼ tsp ground turmeric
- 2 Tbsp olive oil
- ½ small red onion, finely chopped
- 4–6 curry leaves, ripped into small pieces

Cashew Nut Curry
Kaḓju Maluwa

I can recall the first time I had cashew nut curry—the cashews had been plucked fresh from the trees and husked for cooking. They almost melted in my mouth, something Sri Lankans would call *kiri caju* (literally, milk cashews). The natural creaminess of the cashews blended with coconut milk and spices is delicious. Serve with black pork curry (page 119) and tempered snake beans (page 87).

In the first 30–35 minutes of cooking, you may have to add some extra (hot) water. If so, add ¼ cup at a time.

Gently stir the cashews with a wooden spoon while cooking; otherwise the nuts will chip or break. Alternatively, use a pot with two handles so that you can periodically shake the pot to mix the ingredients (see page 34).

Using a small, sharp paring knife, split open any whole cashew nuts. The cashews should be white in colour. Discard any that are greyish. Place the cashews in a medium-size pot.

Add the onion, curry leaves, *pandanus* leaf, salt, cardamom pods, paprika, curry powder, turmeric, and cayenne. Add just enough water to cover the cashew nuts. Cover and bring to a boil over medium heat. Let cook until the cashews are soft and cooked through, approximately 30 minutes. If the water is absorbed sooner than this, add a splash of hot water as needed.

Add the coconut milk and more salt if desired. Swirl to combine, and cook slowly over low heat for another 30–35 minutes. Remove from the heat and let stand for 10 minutes before serving.

Serves 4–6

- ½ lb unsalted, raw cashew nuts (soaked overnight in water)
- ¼ small red onion, chopped finely
- 7 curry leaves, ripped into small pieces
- 1-inch-long piece of *pandanus* leaf, fresh or frozen
- 1 tsp fine sea salt, or to taste
- 2 cardamom pods
- ½ tsp paprika
- ½ tsp unroasted curry powder (page 31)
- ¼ tsp ground turmeric
- ¼ tsp cayenne powder
- ¾ cup coconut milk

Raw cashews take some time to cook through. To quicken the process, I recommend soaking them in a bowl of water for a minimum of 2 hours, but preferably overnight. Drain and rinse before using.

Yellow Dal with/without Spinach
Parippu/Nivithi Parippu

This dal recipe is my favourite lentil curry and uses split red lentils. Traditionally, dal recipes use coconut milk, but full-fat cow's milk is a fine substitute for this recipe—in fact, it's what my mother used when I was a child, as we ate this often during the week. It is common to add fresh spinach to this dish to increase the nutritional value and to add some colour, but that is optional. This recipe is mild and has a wholesome taste. It pairs well with cucumber salad (page 135), parsley *sambola* (page 145), and a fried egg.

Place the lentils, chili (if using), and 1½ cups of water in a pot over high heat. Bring to a boil, immediately turn down the heat to medium, and continue cooking, uncovered, at a steady simmer for 15 minutes. Skim off any froth with a spoon and stir occasionally.

If you see the water is dissipating but the lentils are not fully cooked, add ¼ cup boiling water at a time. You may find it handy to have a kettle of boiled water next to you for this purpose.

About 10 minutes into cooking, stir in the turmeric and then the milk. (You may add a little more milk if preferred.) Add the onion and salt. (Don't be surprised if you find you have to add quite a bit.) Let simmer on medium-low heat for 5 to 10 minutes, or until the lentils are cooked through. (They should be firm but soft.) In terms of the consistency, you want enough liquid so that there is some gravy, but you don't want it to be soupy.

If you are using the spinach, add it now (either whole leaves or chopped in half) and stir into the cooked lentils. Squeeze the lime juice into the dal, and remove the pot from the heat. Stir, cover, and let sit for few minutes prior to serving.

Serves 4–6

1 cup split red lentils, washed

1 small whole green (Thai) chili (optional)

¼ tsp ground turmeric

Approximately ¼ cup coconut milk or full-fat cow's milk

¼ small red or yellow onion, finely chopped

1½–2 tsp fine sea salt, or to taste

½ small bunch of fresh baby spinach, stems removed (optional)

1 small lime wedge (yielding about 1 tsp juice)

Chili Pepper Dal
Parippu Mirisata

This spicy and rustic dal curry is perfect with coconut roti (page 59), beef curry (page 115), good company, and your favourite beverage!

❧

This is meant to be very spicy, but you may wish to reduce the amount of chili (cayenne and crushed chili flakes) at first. You can then adjust the seasoning to your liking as you become more familiar with the recipe.

    Place the lentils in a large bowl. Add half the chopped onion or shallots, the paprika, curry powder, cayenne, turmeric, and salt to taste, and mix to combine.

    Add the oil to a frying pan over high heat. When the oil is hot, add the remaining onion or shallots and temper (page 42).

    When the onion or shallots are golden, add the curry leaves, *pandanus* leaf, and chili flakes, stirring frequently until fragrant and taking care that they don't burn. Add the dal mixture and fry, stirring constantly, until the spices are aromatic and browned, about 1 minute.

    Add 1½ cups of water, bring to a simmer, cover, turn down the heat to medium-low, and let cook, stirring occasionally, until the dal is thoroughly cooked, about 20 minutes. You may need to add more boiling water. If so, add ¼ cup at a time.

    Squeeze the lime wedge over top of the curry. Stir and remove from the heat. Serve immediately.

Serves 4–6

- 1 cup dry split red lentils, washed
- ¼ small red onion or 4 shallots, chopped, divided
- ½ tsp paprika
- ½ tsp unroasted curry powder (page 31)
- ½ tsp cayenne powder
- ¼ tsp ground turmeric
- 1½–2 tsp fine sea salt, or to taste
- 2 Tbsp olive oil
- 4–6 curry leaves, ripped into small pieces
- 1-inch-long piece of *pandanus* leaf, fresh or frozen
- ½ tsp crushed chili flakes
- 1 small lime wedge (yielding about 1 tsp juice)

Mung Bean Curry
Mung Ata Maluwa

The first time I tried mung beans was when my mother made mung bean *kiri bath*. The milk rice was speckled with these small green seeds. Mung beans, which are actually legumes rather than beans and are also known as green *gram*, have a slightly sweet taste, which makes them easy to eat. My mother was also partial to cooking green mung beans rather simply, with only a bit of seasoning. This recipe uses skinned mung beans, which reveals their yellow colour. This goes nicely with coconut *sambol* (page 152), bitter gourd *sambola* (page 141), and fried pork with onions and banana peppers (page 121).

Place the mung beans in a medium-size pot. Add the turmeric, paprika, and cayenne, and mix to combine.

Add the onion, curry leaves, and salt, and mix well.

Add enough water to completely cover the mung bean mixture. Bring to a simmer over medium heat, cover and let cook, stirring occasionally, for 10 minutes. You may need to add more boiling water as the mung beans cook. If so, add ¼ cup at a time.

Stir in the coconut milk. Add more salt to taste if needed.

Turn down the heat to low and let simmer until the mung beans are cooked through. Cooking time is approximately 25 minutes. (The mung beans should be tender but should still hold their shape and not be mushy.)

Serves 4–6

1 cup dry skinned mung beans, washed

1 tsp ground turmeric

1 tsp paprika

¼ tsp cayenne powder

¼ small red onion, chopped

4–6 curry leaves, ripped into small pieces

1 tsp fine sea salt, or to taste

½ cup coconut milk

Roasted Mung Bean Curry
Badthupa Moong Ata

This roasted mung bean recipe is spicy and hearty. Serve with plain white rice, kale *mallum* (page 150) or parsley salad (page 145) and white fish curry (page 127).

❧

In a wide, ungreased frying pan over high heat, roast the mung beans until golden. Shake the pan to encourage even browning, and stir them back and forth with a wooden spoon while they roast. (Some of the beans will roast faster than others to a dark brown, but that's fine.) Pour into a bowl and set aside to cool.

Once cooled, wash the roasted mung beans under cold running water. Put them in a pot and add enough cold water to just cover them. Mix in the onion, curry leaves, *pandanus* leaf, paprika, turmeric, cayenne, and salt to taste.

Cover and let cook over medium heat, stirring occasionally, for 25 minutes. You may need to add more boiling water. If so, add ¼ cup at a time.

Stir in the coconut milk and add more salt to taste, if needed. Turn down the heat to low and let simmer, covered, for another 5 minutes or until the mung beans are cooked through.

Serves 4–6

- 1½ cups dry, skinned mung beans, unwashed
- ¼ small red onion, chopped
- 4 curry leaves, ripped into small pieces
- 1-inch-long piece of *pandanus* leaf, fresh or frozen
- 1½ tsp paprika
- 1 tsp ground turmeric
- 1 tsp cayenne powder
- 1 tsp fine sea salt, or to taste
- 3 Tbsp coconut milk

A KOOMERIAH ELEPHANT AND A MEERGA.
(High caste.) (Low caste.)
(After G. P. Sanderson.)

Meat and Poultry Dishes

Chicken Curry
Kukul Mas Curry

This chicken curry is definitely on my top five list of favourite comfort foods. The secret is in the sauce, as they say, and the roasted curry powder is essential. This dish is delicious with white rice or coconut roti (page 59), white potato curry (page 65), and cucumber salad village-style (page 138).

This recipe can be easily doubled. Simply double all the ingredients, using a mix of drumsticks and thighs, and increase the marinating time to between 2 hours and overnight.

Wash your hands extra thoroughly after you've used them to mix in the cayenne and the other spices with the chicken.

Skin and wash the chicken, and trim off the fat. Pat dry with paper towels. Cut the chicken thighs (along the bone) into two or three pieces.

In a large bowl, place the chicken, paprika, curry powder, cayenne, turmeric, pepper, garlic, ginger, half the onion, curry leaves, *pandanus* leaf, and salt. Squeeze the lime wedge over top and combine the ingredients with your hands.

Cover and let marinate for 15 minutes at room temperature or 30 minutes in the fridge. (Let the chicken return to room temperature before cooking if you marinate it in the fridge.)

In a large pot, heat the oil over high heat. Add first the remaining onion. Fry until the onion is turning golden brown and then add the chili to temper (see page 42). Add the tomato and sauté, stirring, until the tomato has softened, about 30 seconds to 1 minute.

Add the chicken mixture, stir, cover, turn the heat down to medium, and let cook, stirring occasionally, until the chicken releases its natural juices, approximately 5 minutes. Add the coconut milk mixed with water to the chicken. The coconut milk will reach a rapid simmer almost as soon as it is added. Turn the heat down to low, cover, and continue cooking on a slow simmer for 1 hour. Check and stir periodically to see if more coconut milk or water are required. If so, add 2 Tbsp of either at a time.

Turn off the heat and let stand for 10 to 15 minutes before serving. Remove the *pandanus* leaf before serving.

Serves 4–6

- 1–1¼ lb bone-in chicken thighs (3–4 thighs)
- 1½ tsp paprika
- 1 heaping tsp roasted curry powder (page 31)
- ¼ tsp cayenne powder
- ⅛ tsp ground turmeric
- ½ tsp ground black pepper
- 1 garlic clove, finely grated
- 1½–2-inch piece of fresh ginger, peeled and finely grated
- ½ cup chopped small red onion, divided
- 4 curry leaves, ripped into small pieces
- 1-inch-wide piece of *pandanus* leaf, fresh or frozen
- 1 tsp fine sea salt
- 1 small lime wedge (yielding about 1 tsp juice)
- 2 Tbsp olive oil
- 1 Tbsp finely chopped Roma tomato
- 1 green (Thai) chili, cut in half
- ½ cup coconut milk mixed with ¼ cup water

Keep a slow simmer to bring out the flavours of the spices and make the chicken soft and tender.

Boiled Eggs with Coconut Milk
Biththara Kiri Hothi

Coconut milk gravy, or *kiri hothi* as it is called in Sinhala, is traditionally served with Sri Lankan string hoppers. The recipe typically includes boiled eggs for added protein, as string hoppers are usually served for breakfast. You can buy premade frozen string hoppers or *idiappam* in Indian food markets. Enjoy this with white rice, coconut roti (page 59), vermicelli noodles, or string hoppers with some coconut *sambol* (page 152) for a quick and easy breakfast or a light weeknight meal.

In a large pot over medium-high heat, place the onion, curry leaves, *pandanus* leaf, chili, salt, turmeric, fenugreek, and coconut milk. Bring to a boil, then turn the heat down to low and let simmer for 5–10 minutes. Stir and add more salt, if preferred.

Meanwhile, slice each egg vertically halfway down toward its centre, taking care not to slice the whole way through. Add the eggs to the milk while it is simmering.

Remove from the heat. Squeeze the lime wedge over the milk and gently stir to combine. Eggs may be halved during serving.

Serves 4

½ small red onion, finely chopped

4–6 curry leaves, ripped into small pieces

1½-inch-wide piece of *pandanus* leaf, fresh or frozen

1 green (Thai) chili, cut diagonally into small pieces (optional)

½ tsp salt, or to taste

⅛ tsp ground turmeric

Pinch of fenugreek seeds

1¼ cups coconut milk

4 hard-boiled eggs, shells removed

1 small lime wedge (yielding about 1 tsp juice)

Beef Curry
Harak Mas Curry

My mother recalls that after Sri Lankan New Year in April, everyone would head up to Nuwara Eliya to see the car and horse races and partake in the festivities. More importantly, her brother would host large parties and the beef curry he served, as she remembers it, was unlike any other.

The special flavour of this beef curry is due to the careful addition of tamarind and lemon grass.

Slice the beef into evenly sized pieces about 1½-inches-long and 1-inch-wide and place them in a large bowl. Add the roasted curry powder, cayenne, paprika, turmeric, garlic, ginger, tamarind, half the Thai chili, curry leaves, *pandanus* leaf, and lemon grass and salt. Combine with your hands (see page 34) to coat all the pieces, cover, and let marinate for 15 to 20 minutes at room temperature or 30 minutes in the fridge. (Let the beef return to room temperature before cooking if you marinate it in the fridge.)

In a large pot, heat the oil over high heat. Add the onion and the remaining chili and temper (see page 42) until the onion is golden brown. Then add the chopped tomato, and stir for another minute, or until the tomato has softened.

Mix in the beef, turn down the heat to medium-high, and cook, covered, until the beef's natural juices are released, approximately 5 minutes, stirring occasionally. Then add enough water to just cover the beef.

Turn down the heat to low, cover, and let cook for 30 minutes, stirring occasionally (but do not overstir).

Taste the gravy and adjust salt, as desired. Stir in 3 Tbsp of coconut milk and continue cooking, partially covered if you wish to reduce the gravy slightly, for another 30 minutes on low heat. Periodically check on the consistency. You may want to add another 1 Tbsp of coconut milk or a little water to adjust the gravy to your desired consistency.

Turn off the heat and let stand on the stovetop for 10 to 15 minutes before serving. Remove the *pandanus* leaf before serving.

Serves 4

- 1–1¼ lb beef (rump or chuck roast)
- 2 heaping teaspoons roasted curry powder (page 31)
- ½ tsp cayenne powder
- 1½–2 tsp paprika
- Pinch of ground tumeric
- 2 fresh garlic cloves, peeled and crushed
- 1½–2 inch piece of fresh ginger, peeled and finely grated
- ½ tsp tamarind paste
- 1 green (Thai) chili, halved, divided
- 5–7 curry leaves, ripped into small pieces
- 2-inch-wide piece of *pandanus* leaf
- 1-inch piece of lemon grass
- 1 tsp fine sea salt, or to taste
- 2 Tbsp olive oil
- ½ small red onion, finely chopped
- ½ cup chopped Roma tomato
- 3 Tbsp–¼ cup coconut milk

Peppered Beef with Coconut Milk and Mustard Seed

Harak Mas Gam Miris Pol Kiri Badthum

In this recipe, the beef is marinated in a healthy sprinkling of black pepper and cooked in a blend of ground mustard seeds, vinegar, and coconut milk. You will appreciate some milder dishes alongside this spicy, tangy, savoury beef to balance out the flavours. Enjoy with plain white rice, okra curry (page 83) or yellow dal curry (page 101), or include it as one of the curries in rice and curries packed in banana leaves (page 61).

The ground black pepper adds quite a kick to this dish. If you prefer less heat, begin with 1 tsp and work your way up.

Thinly slice the beef into approximately 2-inch-long and 1-inch-wide strips and place them in a bowl. Add the garlic, ginger, turmeric, pepper, salt, and 1 Tbsp of oil and the 1 Tbsp of vinegar.

Mix everything together, cover and let marinate in the fridge for 30 minutes. (Let the beef return to room temperature before cooking.)

While the meat is marinating, prepare the coconut milk mixture.

Using a mortar and pestle, finely grind the mustard seeds. Place them in a small bowl, add the 1 tsp vinegar and the coconut milk, and mix well. Set aside.

When the meat is ready to cook, place 3 Tbsp oil in a wide frying pan over medium-high heat. When the oil is hot, temper (see page 42) the curry leaves.

Add the meat to the hot pan, and cook, covered, stirring occasionally, until it has browned. Turn down the heat to medium and let cook, partially covered, for approximately 20 minutes. When the meat begins to release its natural juices, remove the lid and cook for another 10 to 15 minutes to reduce and thicken the liquid.

Add the coconut milk mixture to the meat and mix to combine. Let cook, uncovered, for another 5 minutes over medium heat to allow the flavours to blend. Add the onion and banana pepper, and more salt, if preferred. Slightly cook the onion. (It should be cooked but not mushy.) Turn off the heat and let sit for a few minutes before serving.

Serves 4

- 1–1¼ lb beef (rump or chuck roast, if possible)
- 1 garlic clove, finely grated or chopped
- 1½–2-inch piece of ginger, finely grated
- 1 tsp ground turmeric
- 2 tsp ground black pepper
- 1 tsp fine sea salt, or to taste
- 4 Tbsp olive oil, divided
- 1 Tbsp + 1 tsp white vinegar
- 1 Tbsp black mustard seeds
- ½ cup coconut milk
- 5 curry leaves, ripped into small pieces
- ½ yellow onion, thickly sliced
- 1 banana pepper, thickly sliced into pieces on the diagonal

If you don't have a mortar and pestle, use a spice or coffee grinder to grind the mustard seeds.

Black Pork Curry
Kalu Uru Mas Curry

Enough cannot be said of the Sri Lankan delicacy black pork curry. It is a delicious and truly flavourful dish, and, like many recipes in this book, every family has their own generational recipe. This recipe may not be one you learn overnight. It is, however, worthy of the time and effort you'll put into preparing it. Its spiciness comes from the black pepper and its black colour from the roasted curry powder and roasted coconut.

※

Start by dry-roasting the rice and coconut. Set a stainless-steel pan over high heat. When the pan is hot, add the rice. Watch the rice closely, as the heat will make the grains begin to pop. Shake the pan to help roast the grains evenly, to quicken the popping, and to avoid burning.

When the grains are evenly roasted and browned, pour them onto a plate or into a bowl and set aside to cool.

Set the pan back over high heat. Add the coconut to the pan.

Using the back of a fork or spoon, lightly press the coconut into the pan to quicken the roasting. Working quickly, stir the coconut around in the pan and shake the pan to help the pieces roast evenly.

When the coconut is almost black (but not burnt) transfer it to a separate dish and set aside to cool. (There may be some pieces that are still whitish in colour.)

Using a mortar and pestle, grind half of the roasted rice grains. Add the pepper (or whole peppercorns) and continue grinding until the rice looks like fine crumbs. Pour into a bowl and set aside.

Pour the coconut into the mortar and pound it until it looks like fine coffee grounds. If the coconut is fresh, there will be a bit of oil. Set aside.

Cut the pork and its fat into 1-inch chunks and place them in a pot. Add the *goraka* (or lemon juice), onion, garlic, ginger, curry leaves, curry powder, paprika, cayenne, turmeric, and salt. Add enough cold water to just cover the meat mixture, set the pot over medium-high heat, and cover. Once it has reached a boil, turn down the heat to medium-low and let it cook, covered, for 45 minutes. Check occasionally to see if more salt is needed.

Add the ground rice and coconut mixture to the pork. Mix everything to combine, turn down the heat to low, partially cover, and let simmer for another 15 minutes.

Serves 4

¼ cup unwashed, parboiled white rice (any type of rice)

¼ cup scraped coconut or frozen grated coconut (thawed)

1 tsp ground black pepper or 5 peppercorns

1–1¼ lb boneless pork roast with a fat cap

3–4 pieces dried *goraka* preserved in brine or the juice of 1 small lemon

¼ red onion, finely chopped

3 garlic cloves, peeled and finely chopped or sliced

1½-inch piece of fresh ginger, peeled and finely chopped

6 curry leaves, ripped into small pieces

3½ heaping tsp roasted curry powder

3½ tsp paprika

2 heaping tsp cayenne powder

1 tsp ground turmeric

1½ tsp fine sea salt, or to taste

Fried Pork with Onions and Banana Peppers
Uru Mas Badthum

Enjoy the wonderful aroma of the tempered garlic and ginger in this savoury pork dish, and the kick of heat from the ground black pepper! This is a visually appetizing dish with its light-yellow hue and the glistening onion and banana peppers spooned over top. Enjoy a serving of this dish over some yellow rice (page 53) with a spoonful of eggplant pickle (page 154).

The ground black pepper adds quite a kick to this dish. If you prefer less heat, begin with less than 1 tablespoon.

Thinly slice the pork and its fat into approximately 2-inch-long strips, and place the strips in a bowl.

Add the curry leaves, *pandanus* leaf, pepper, turmeric, and vinegar. Mix everything together, cover, and let marinate in the fridge for 30 minutes. (Let the pork return to room temperature before cooking.)

Set a wide frying pan over high heat and add the oil. When the oil is hot, add the garlic and ginger and fry just until lightly browned.

Add the pork, with its marinade, to the pan and stir to combine with the garlic and ginger. Turn the heat down to medium-low and let cook, covered, for about 15 minutes, stirring occasionally for even browning. (The meat will release its own juices.)

Turn the heat down to low and continue frying for another 5 minutes, uncovered, until the pieces are browned and slightly crisp.

Add the sliced onion and banana pepper, squeeze the lime wedge over top, and increase the heat to medium-high. Fry until the onion is translucent, approximately 3 minutes, then turn off the heat.

Serves 4

- 1–1¼ lb pork shoulder with fat cap
- 5–6 curry leaves, ripped into small pieces
- 1-inch piece of *pandanus* leaf
- 1 heaping Tbsp ground black pepper
- 1 tsp ground turmeric
- 1 Tbsp white vinegar
- 3 Tbsp olive oil
- 2 garlic cloves, finely chopped
- 1-inch piece of fresh ginger, peeled and finely chopped
- ½ red or yellow onion, cut into thick slices
- 1 banana pepper, deseeded, cut on the diagonal into thick slices
- 1 small lime wedge (yielding about 1 tsp juice)

Seafood Dishes

Devilled Prawns
Isso Badthum

In Sri Lanka, a devilled dish is most often equated with "very hot!" This may be true, but *devilling* is also a method of cooking in which the main ingredient (vegetable, fruit, or protein) is marinated with chili (chili sauce or ground or crushed chilies) and often sautéed with garlic and ginger. Reminiscent of Portuguese influences with a modern fusion of Asian flavours, devilled dishes often include tomatoes, capsicums, and onion. I love that this dish has a bit of sweetness due to the caramelizing of ingredients at the end of cooking. Serve with yellow rice (page 53), tempered snake beans (page 87), yellow dal with/without spinach (page 101), or white potato curry (page 65).

Place the prawns, half the garlic, ginger, salt, ½ tsp of the chili flakes, lime juice, and chili paste in a bowl. Mix together, cover, and let marinate in the fridge for 30 minutes.

Place the oil in a wide frying pan set over medium-high heat, and fry the remaining garlic and ½ tsp chili flakes to release their aroma. Add the prawns and, stirring constantly, cook for about 5 minutes.

Add the sugar, stirring quickly to coat the prawns. When the prawns are nicely browned, add the onion, tomato (if using), and capsicum (or banana pepper). Adjust salt. Stir to combine and let cook for another minute or two. Finish by sprinkling the green scallions over top, give it all a quick stir, remove from the heat, and serve right away.

Serves 4

- ½ lb fresh large prawns (see page 126), shelled or unshelled, tails left on, and deveined
- 2 garlic cloves, finely grated, divided
- 2-inch piece of fresh ginger, peeled and finely grated
- 1 tsp fine sea salt, or to taste
- 1 tsp chili flakes, divided
- 1 Tbsp lime juice
- 1 tsp chili paste
- 2 Tbsp olive oil
- 1 tsp granulated sugar
- ½ red onion, sliced
- 1 Roma tomato, cubed (optional)
- 1 red bell pepper or banana pepper, deseeded and sliced
- 3 green scallions, cut diagonally into long pieces

Prawn Curry
Isso Curry

This shrimp curry is a simple yet fragrant dish that can be easily prepared during weeknights and will go nicely with chili pepper dal (page 103), coconut roti (page 59), vermicelli noodles, or string hoppers.

In Sri Lanka, this recipe calls for prawns and is called prawn curry. Large shrimp are more easily found in North American grocery stores and are an acceptable substitute.

The lemon grass makes a notable difference to the flavour, so if you are not used to cooking with it, you may wish to use a little less to begin with.

To clean the shellfish, place them in a bowl, squeeze the juice from a lemon wedge over top, and then place the bowl under cold, running water to clean the prawns.

Place the prawns, salt, turmeric, paprika, cayenne, roasted curry powder, chili flakes, and lime juice in a bowl. Mix to combine, cover, and marinate in the fridge for 30 minutes.

Place the oil in a pot over high heat. When the oil is hot, add the onion and cook, stirring, until just translucent. Add the garlic, ginger, lemon grass, curry leaves, and *pandanus* leaf and stir to release their aromas for 1 to 2 minutes. Add the prawns, stir with the other ingredients for a few seconds, then add ½ cup water and coconut milk. Stir to combine. When the mixture has reached a rapid simmer, turn down the heat to medium-low, and let cook, uncovered, for 4 or 5 minutes.

Turn the heat down to low and let simmer for another 2 to 3 minutes, stirring occasionally. Add salt as desired. Remove the *pandanus* leaf before serving.

Serves 4–6

½ lb fresh prawns, rinsed with cold water and lemon (see note), shelled (optional) and deveined

1 tsp fine sea salt

½ tsp ground turmeric

½ tsp paprika

½ tsp cayenne powder

½ tsp roasted curry powder (page 31)

Pinch of dried chili flakes

1 Tbsp lime juice

2 Tbsp olive oil

½ small white onion, diced

2 garlic cloves, finely chopped

1-inch piece of fresh ginger, peeled and sliced

1-inch piece of lemon grass

5–7 curry leaves, ripped into small pieces

2-inch-wide piece of *pandanus* leaf, fresh or frozen

¼ cup coconut milk

If you don't have time to properly clean and devein shrimp, use frozen, pre-peeled and deveined shrimp.

White Fish Curry
Suthu Malu Curry

I can recall being a young girl in Sri Lanka and seeing the traditional method of stilt fishing, where fishermen skillfully sit on high poles fixed to the floor of the ocean's shallow waters to catch fish. It was a stunning sight, and it made me appreciate even more a meal with fresh fish. Sri Lanka has an unsurpassed variety of fresh fish and seafood. This simple fish recipe is delicious with a plate of white steaming rice, winter squash curry (page 73), beetroot curry (page 71), and kale *mallum* (page 150).

A pinch or ¼ tsp of turmeric is added to give this dish a very light yellow colour.

Cut the fish into 1½-inch cubes. Drizzle the lemon juice over top (making sure to hold back the seeds), followed by a few of the curry leaves, the curry powder, pepper, cayenne, turmeric, fenugreek, and salt to taste. Gently mix with your hands to combine.

In a large saucepan over medium-high heat, warm the oil and temper (see page 42) the remaining curry leaves and the onion. Add the green chili, and lightly brown it.

Add the fish, gently mix with the tempered ingredients, and then, without overlapping the pieces, add ¼ cup water and let cook, uncovered, until the liquid reaches a soft boil. Mix in the coconut milk.

Turn the heat down to low and cook, uncovered, until the fish is cooked through (the flesh will become opaque and will easily flake), approximately 10 minutes. Adjust the salt to taste before serving.

Serves 4

1–1¼ lb boneless halibut steak (or preferred white fish), washed and skinned

Juice of ½ lemon

4–6 whole curry leaves, divided

1½ tsp unroasted curry powder (page 31)

¼ tsp black pepper

Pinch of cayenne powder

Pinch of ground turmeric

Pinch of fenugreek seeds

1 tsp fine sea salt, or to taste

2 Tbsp olive oil

½ cup red onion, chopped

1 whole green (Thai) chili

1 cup + 2 Tbsp coconut milk

Sour Fish Curry
Ambul Thiyal

Sour fish curry is a classic Sri Lankan delicacy. If you have never tried this before, don't let the English translation of its name dissuade you. It is delicious, and probably one of the most unique dishes in this book for its combination of ingredients, whose flavours are enhanced by slow cooking.

The ingredient that gives this recipe its particular sour flavour is the *goraka* (see page 38), which is ground to a paste with black pepper and smothered over delicate pieces of fresh fish. Traditionally, the seasoned fish is cooked in a clay pot lined with banana leaves and over an open hearth until the fish is quite dry. As this is not possible in a Western kitchen, my mother adapted this recipe, so that the fish bakes slowly in the oven. This is traditionally served for breakfast but is lovely for dinner with brown rice, beetroot curry (page 71), and winter squash curry (page 73).

Choose fresh fish with firm flesh and a mild flavour. I recommend fresh halibut for this curry because of its neutral flavour, which balances well with the stronger seasonings in this dish. Tuna would also work well.

Serves 4–6

- 2 lb halibut steaks (preferably with bones)
- 7 pieces of *goraka* in brine, drained and chopped
- 2 Tbsp ground black pepper
- 1-inch piece of ginger, finely sliced
- Pinch of turmeric
- 1½ tsp fine sea salt, or to taste
- 2 Tbsp olive oil
- ½ large red onion, chopped
- 16–18 curry leaves
- 2 (each 2 inches wide) pieces of *pandanus* leaf, fresh or frozen
- 2 green (Thai) chilies

Preheat the oven to 375°F.

Remove the skin of the fish, then rinse the fish steaks under cold running water. Cut the steaks into approximately 2-inch cubes. Place them in a large bowl and set aside.

Using a mortar and pestle, grind the *goraka* and black pepper into a paste. Add the *goraka* paste, the ginger, turmeric, a good amount of salt, and ¼ cup of water to the fish. Using your hands, gently mix to combine, taking care not to break the flesh of the fish. Set aside.

In a wide saucepan over medium-high heat, heat the oil and fry the onion until just beginning to brown. Add the curry leaves, *pandanus* leaf, and chilies, and fry slightly to release their flavours, approximately 1 minute. Add the fish to the pan and mix gently, just to combine all the ingredients.

Place the fish pieces (so that they are not overlapping) in a casserole dish that has been lightly oiled or lined with cleaned banana leaves (see page 39). Spoon any remaining tempered onion mixture over top of the fish.

Cover with aluminum foil and bake on the centre rack of the oven for 25 minutes.

Remove the foil and continue baking until almost all the juices have been absorbed and the fish is dry in texture, approximately 20 to 25 minutes.

Crab Curry
Kakuluwo Curry

Fresh crab curry is without a doubt an absolute favourite of Sri Lankans, no matter what region of the country they are from. The flavour of this curry is enhanced by the addition of drumstick (*moringa*) leaves, which can be found in Asian markets. Serve with ghee rice (page 57).

Place the crab meat in a bowl and squeeze the lemon over top.

Add the paprika, curry powder, cayenne, turmeric, fenugreek, and salt to taste. Mix to combine, cover, and marinate in the fridge for 30 minutes to 1 hour.

Heat the oil in a frying pan over medium-high heat and temper (see page 42) the onion until browned. Add the garlic, ginger, and chili, and stir just to release flavours. Add the crab, with its marinade, and stir to combine. Add the *moringa* leaves, ½ cup of water, and coconut milk, and stir to combine.

Turn the heat down to its lowest setting and let simmer gently, uncovered, for 5 to 10 minutes. Serve right away.

Serves 4–6

1 lb cooked crabmeat

¼ lemon

1 tsp paprika

½ tsp roasted curry powder (page 31)

½ tsp cayenne powder

½ tsp ground turmeric

Pinch of fenugreek seeds

1 tsp fine sea salt, or to taste

2 Tbsp vegetable oil

1 small red onion, roughly chopped

2 garlic cloves, finely grated

1½-inch piece of ginger, finely grated

1 whole green (Thai) chili

1 cup *moringa* leaves, rinsed in cold water and removed from stems

½ cup water

¼ cup + 2 Tbsp coconut milk

You may use 1 lb of canned pasteurized blue lump crab meat, available at most North American grocery stores.

Salads

Cucumber Salad
Pipinna Sambola

This salad is a staple dish in my household—and with its being such a dainty dish, it's a surprise that my husband is the one who often requests it! I am not sure why it is so satisfying, but I'm inclined to think it's its simplicity. The few ingredients of this salad combine to create a cool, refreshing mix of flavours. When I used to watch my mother prepare this, I noticed that she made a special effort to very thinly slice the cucumber. This does make a difference to the taste, texture, and flavour. The cucumber nicely absorbs the lime dressing and delicately complements rice and a variety of curries (especially meat curries with robust flavours).

While you can prep and chop the ingredients ahead of time, it is best to add the dressing just prior to serving, so the vegetables maintain their crunch.

Serves 4

- 1 field or English cucumber, peeled
- ½ small red or white onion
- ½ green (Thai) chili
- ½–1 tsp fine sea salt, or to taste
- ¼ tsp ground black pepper
- 1 small lime wedge (yielding about 1 tsp juice)

Getting the right balance of lime and salt is what makes this salad so tasty, especially since this recipe requires an ample amount of both. The generous amount of lime juice complements and equalizes the extra salt.

Thinly slice the cucumber and place the slices in a bowl. Thinly slice the onion, separate out the rings or slices, and add to the cucumber.

Thinly slice the green chili on the diagonal and add to the cucumber.

Add the salt and pepper, squeeze the lime wedge over top, and combine all the ingredients with your hands. Taste and adjust the salt if necessary. Serve right away.

Tomato, Cucumber, and Red Onion Salad

Thakkali, Pipinna, Rathu Lunu Salada

This eye-catching salad is perfect for large dinner parties and is a refreshing complement to rice and curries. The trick is in the presentation—it is a flat, layered salad with fresh sliced vegetables sitting on top of a bed of crisp ruffled lettuce, so taking a bit of extra time to find just the right ingredients is worth the effort. It is finished with a light dressing and a sprinkling of black pepper.

This salad may be prepped in advance with the vegetables kept sliced and ready in the fridge in containers.

Select firm ripe tomatoes that are uniform in their roundness and size. As you slice the tomatoes, the evenly sized slices will lie nicely next to each other, creating visual balance.

Field cucumbers tend to be slightly wider than English ones, so visually they pair well against the tomatoes and onion rings when sliced.

Either red or white onions work for this salad, but the colour of red onions makes this salad even more appealing.

Use a head of green leaf lettuce or a variety of lettuces with crisp, curly leaves.

If you're using a wide serving dish, you might need to increase the number of tomatoes for even coverage of the dish.

Using a sharp knife, thinly slice the tomatoes into rounds and then set aside. Thinly slice the cucumbers into rounds and set aside.

Thinly slice the onion, separate out the slices, and set aside.

Using a shallow round serving dish or plate, arrange enough lettuce leaves to cover the face of the dish, with the frilly tips of the lettuce lining the edge of the dish.

Beginning from below the frilly edge of the lettuce, arrange the tomatoes around the outer edge in a circle, gently overlapping. Then arrange a circle of onion over the tomatoes, then the cucumbers below the onion. Continue this pattern until you arrive at the centre. Use a single tomato or cucumber slice to fill the centre space. Tuck any remaining onion rings into the salad wherever they look good.

For the dressing, whisk together the vinegar, lime juice, sugar, salt, and pepper. Spoon the dressing over the salad just before serving and finish with a light sprinkling of freshly ground black pepper.

Serves 6

SALAD

4 firm, round, vine-ripened red tomatoes, stems removed

1–1½ medium field cucumbers, peeled

1–2 red onion

1 head of green leaf lettuce, stems trimmed

VINEGAR DRESSING

¼ cup white vinegar

1 Tbsp lime juice

1 tsp granulated sugar

½ tsp fine sea salt

¼ tsp ground black pepper

Cucumber Salad Village-Style
Gama Pipinna Sambola

This is a rustic version of cucumber salad, but just as delicious. Try it with red or brown rice, young jackfruit curry (page 91) or white fish curry (page 127), beetroot curry (page 71), and roasted mung bean curry (page 105).

Thinly slice the cucumbers and place them in a bowl. Add the ground mustard seeds, ginger, salt to taste, coconut milk, and lime juice. Combine with a spoon. Taste and adjust the salt. Serve right away.

Serves 4

1½ field cucumbers, peeled

1 Tbsp black mustard seeds, freshly ground

1 tsp finely sliced fresh ginger

½ tsp fine sea salt, or to taste

¼ cup coconut milk

1 Tbsp lime juice

Carrot Slaw
Carrot Sambola

This refreshing slaw is so delicious and easy to prepare and is a nice departure from the usual greens that so many of us associate with salads. Enjoy with white rice, chicken curry (page 111), green bean white curry (page 85), and kale *mallum* (page 150).

Combine all the ingredients in a bowl with your hands.

Serves 4–6

1 lb (2–3 medium-size) carrots, peeled and finely grated

2 green (Thai) chilies, finely sliced

¼ small red onion, peeled and finely chopped

1 Tbsp finely scraped coconut (either fresh, frozen, or desiccated, see page 34)

½ tsp fine sea salt, or to taste

1 Tbsp lime juice

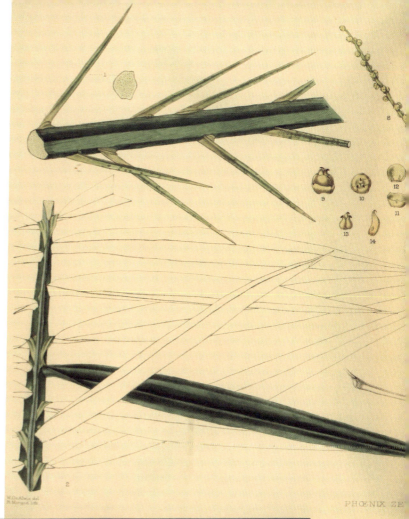

Bitter Gourd Salad
Karavila (Badthala) Sambola

While Sri Lanka's upcountry vegetables include crops such as cabbage, carrots, beetroots, cauliflower, and peppers, the low country (plains) is known for vegetables such as eggplant, pumpkins, melons, cucumbers, and gourds. Bitter gourds (sometimes called bitter melon) are commonly available in Asian and Indian stores and are worth trying if you haven't already. They almost have the shape of a small swollen cucumber with a pointed bumpy skin and a skinny tail. Despite the name, there is no trace of bitterness in this salad. Once you've tried it, you will be inclined to make it again! Serve with brown rice, kale *mallum* (page 150), a dal curry, and a fried egg.

Serves 4

- 1 lb (approximately 2–3 large) bitter gourds, ends trimmed
- Approximately 4 cups vegetable oil for frying
- ½ small red onion
- ½ green (Thai) chili
- 1 tsp fine sea salt, or to taste
- ½ lime

Using a sharp knife, lightly skim the tips of the ridges of the bitter gourds to remove any darkened edges. Thinly slice the gourds into rounds—aim for slices ¼ inch thick.

Half-fill a medium-size pot with the oil. (You may not need all 4 cups.) Heat the oil on high until it is very hot but not smoking (350°–375 °F). Fry the gourd pieces in small batches, taking care not to overcrowd the pot and gently turning the pieces until their colour changes from bright green to dull green, the ridges are browned, and the interior flesh and seeds are browned. Keep a careful watch so they don't burn or overcook.

Using a slotted spoon, remove the gourd rounds from the pot and set them on a plate that has been covered with paper towels. Using another paper towel, gently pat the pieces to remove any excess oil. Set them aside.

Thinly slice the onion and thinly slice the chili on the diagonal.

When ready to serve, put the fried bitter gourd slices, onion, and chili in a bowl. Sprinkle the salt to taste, and squeeze the lime wedge over top. Mix everything gently with your hands to coat the pieces evenly. Serve right away.

Eggplant Salad
Wambatu (Badthala) Sambola

Instead of deep-frying the eggplant, you can broil it, but the texture and flavour of the deep-fried pieces are what makes this salad so delicious—and they are a nice contrast to the rest of the ingredients. The fried eggplant goes well with the crunchy onion, bell pepper, and tomato, and absorbs the sweet and sour dressing beautifully.

Only add the dressing when you are ready to serve, otherwise the pieces will become soft.

Cut the eggplant into even bite-size pieces. If you are using Japanese or Chinese eggplant, thinly slice them into rounds and then half-moons. If you are using Indian eggplants, thinly slice them into rectangles, approximately 1½ inches long and less than 1 inch wide.

Half-fill a medium-size pot with the oil. (You may not need all 4 cups.) Heat the oil on high until it is very hot but not smoking (350°–375 °F). Fry the eggplant pieces in small batches, taking care not to overcrowd the pot and gently turning the pieces, until the flesh is golden brown, approximately 1 minute. Because the flesh is delicate, you have to keep a careful watch so the eggplant pieces don't burn. Do not overfry.

Using a slotted spoon, remove the pieces of eggplant from the pot and set them on a plate that has been covered with paper towels. Using another paper towel, gently pat the pieces to remove any excess oil. Set them aside.

Thinly slice the red onion and bell pepper, chop the tomato, and thinly slice the green chili on the diagonal. For the dressing, whisk together the vinegar, lime juice (if using), sugar, salt, and pepper.

When ready to serve, put the fried eggplant, onion, bell pepper, tomato, and chili in a bowl. Add the dressing and mix gently with your hands to coat the pieces evenly. Serve right away.

Serves 4–6

SALAD

1 lb eggplant (Japanese, Chinese, or Indian), stems removed

Approximately 4 cups vegetable oil for frying

½ small red onion

½ red or orange bell pepper, deseeded

½ small red Roma tomato

½ green (Thai) chili

DRESSING

¼ cup white vinegar

Juice of ¼ small lime (optional)

1 tsp granulated sugar

½ tsp fine sea salt, or to taste

¼ tsp ground black pepper

Parsley Salad
Parsley Sambola

The traditional recipe for this *sambola* uses pennywort, also called *gotukola*. *Gotukola* is nutritious with a mild taste. However, watercress or parsley also serve as great options for this refreshing salad.

Getting the right balance of lime and salt is key to this sambola. *Experiment a little to find the right amounts for your palate.*

Wash the leaves and cut away the stems of the parsley. Add to a food processor, and pulse until it is very finely chopped (but not minced). Be careful not to overchop the parsley, as this can make it mushy and bitter.

Finely dice the onion and thinly slice the green chili by hand. (Avoid the temptation to just throw them into the food processor.)

Place the parsley, onion, chili, and coconut in a bowl. Squeeze the lime wedge over top and gradually add salt to taste. Combine the ingredients with clean hands or a spoon. Taste and add more lime juice or salt, as needed.

Serves 4–6

1 bunch of fresh parsley, watercress, or pennywort

½ small red onion

1 small green (Thai) chili

¼ cup finely scraped coconut (either fresh, frozen, or desiccated, see page 34)

1 small lime wedge (yielding about 1 tsp juice)

½ tsp fine sea salt, or to taste

Pineapple Salad
Ännasi Salada

This chopped salad is a festive mix of bright colours and varied textures. The refreshing pineapple, cool cucumber, and crunchy bell pepper creates a melange of flavours that helps to balance the heat of spicy dishes and the richness of milk-based curries. It is great for larger parties and a very tasty accompaniment to yellow rice (page 53) and chicken curry (page 111), and other savoury dishes.

※

Slice the pineapple spears into bite-size pieces. Place the pineapple in a bowl large enough to hold all the ingredients.

Dice the cucumber into pieces the same size as the pineapple pieces and add to the pineapple and cucumber.

Finely slice the bell pepper, dice the onion, and chiffonade the mint into paper-like threads (if using), and add to the pineapple.

For the dressing, whisk together the vinegar, sugar, salt, and pepper. Pour over the salad and mix to combine when ready to serve.

Serves 4–6

SALAD

1 small fresh, ripe pineapple, skinned, cored, and sliced into spears (see page 41)

½ medium field cucumber, peeled

½ red bell pepper, deseeded

½–¾ red onion

3–4 mint leaves (optional)

DRESSING

¼ cup white vinegar

1 tsp granulated sugar

½ tsp fine sea salt

¼ tsp ground black pepper + more to taste

Mallum, Sambol, and Pickles

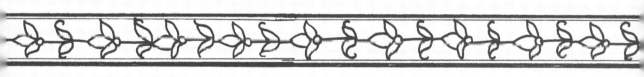

Mallum
Mallum

Mallums are how Sri Lankans eat their "greens." A *mallum* is included in at least one meal every day and is highly nutritious. The raw edible leaves of virtually any plant, and sometimes raw fruits or vegetables, are finely cut, seasoned with a few spices (usually salt, pepper, turmeric) and other ingredients (fresh coconut, chili, and sometimes Maldives fish). Traditionally, the *mallum* is cooked in a dry pan. This is because when a *mallum* is prepared with fresh coconut, little or no oil is needed because of the coconut's natural oil. A little oil is sometimes needed when using frozen or dessicated coconut.

Kale Mallum
Kalē Mallum

One bunch of kale may yield approximately 5 cups once it is finely chopped. While this may seem like a large quantity, it will reduce by about 1 cup once it is pan-fried. The best way to prepare the mallum is to finely chop the kale by hand. If you don't have time, an electric chopper works well, but be careful to not to overchop.

Trim the kale leaves from the stems and discard the stems. Cut the leaves into small pieces so they are easier to place into the electric chopper.

Finely chop the kale (you may have to work in small batches when using an electric chopper) and place it in a bowl. Add the chilies, salt, pepper, and turmeric, and mix to combine.

Heat the oil in a wide, large frying pan over high heat and temper (see page 42) the onion. Turn the heat down to medium-high.

Add the coconut to the pan, and, stirring constantly, mix it with the onion for a couple of minutes. Do not let the coconut brown. Once you smell its aroma being released, add the kale mixture to the pan.

Mix the kale into the coconut and onion. Stirring constantly, cook for 5 to 6 minutes to ensure they don't burn. (You may need to add a little water or a little more oil.) The kale should be soft to the bite, still colourful, and not limp or overcooked. Once it is done, remove the pan from the heat.

Taste and add salt as needed. This *mallum* may be served hot or warm.

Serves 6

- 1 bunch of fresh green kale
- 1½ small green (Thai) chilies, finely sliced
- 1 tsp fine sea salt, or to taste
- ½ tsp ground black pepper
- ¼ tsp ground turmeric
- ½ Tbsp olive oil
- ¼ small red onion, finely chopped
- ⅔ cup finely scraped coconut (either fresh, frozen, or desiccated, see page 34)

Raw Papaya Mallum
Amu Papol Mallum

In a bowl, place ½ cup of the coconut, the onion, chilies, curry leaves, and mustard seeds. Stir to combine.

Using an electric chopper, chop the mixture in batches until it is well ground.

Set a wide, ungreased frying pan over medium heat. Add the remaining 1 cup of coconut, the papaya, salt, pepper, turmeric, and ¼ cup of water.

Once the water has been absorbed, add the ground coconut mixture. Cook, stirring continually, and using quick back-and-forth and folding motions, to evenly cook the ingredients and avoid burning. Add more salt as needed.

When the papaya is tender and soft to the bite, squeeze the lime wedge over top and remove the pan from the heat. Let sit for 5 minutes before serving.

Serves 4–6

1½ cups finely scraped coconut (either fresh, frozen, or desiccated, see page 34), divided

½ small red onion, thinly chopped

3 small green (Thai) chilies, very thinly sliced

4 curry leaves

1½ tsp black mustard seeds

2 cups grated unripened papaya (about ½ large unripened papaya)

½ tsp fine sea salt, or to taste

¼ tsp ground black pepper

¼ tsp ground turmeric

1 small lime wedge (yielding about 1 tsp juice)

Kale Mallum
(recipe on facing page)

Sambol
Sambol

Coconut Sambol
Pol Sambol

I recall my father being in the kitchen and preparing a large bowl of his freshly scraped coconut *sambol*—his sleeves rolled up, and his hands working away at making sure that all the ingredients and the coconut were well combined, sprinkling in the chili and the Maldives fish. A final squeeze of lime would finish the dish.

Coconut *sambol* is one of my favourite Sri Lankan treats, although it is really a side dish for main grains such as string hoppers, *hoppers*, coconut roti (page 59), and milk rice (page 51). Coconut *sambol* is a striking dish because of its orange hue—a result of the addition of cayenne and/or paprika.

Place the coconut, onion, cayenne, paprika, Maldives fish (if using), and salt in a large bowl. Using your hands, mix all the ingredients together to ensure all of the coconut is coated. Taste and adjust the salt. Add the lime juice over everything, mix again to combine, and taste, adding more lime juice if preferred. Serve fresh.

The sambol *preparation is a perfect way to take advantage of the island's resplendent variety of fruits and vegetables.* Sambol *is a mixed preparation of finely cut raw fruit or vegetables combined with chili, lime, sometimes dried Maldives fish or dried prawn, and usually a generous seasoning of salt. Some* sambols *may be tempered with additional condiments and/or spices. Common preparations are coconut* sambol *and onion chili* sambol. *However, other fruits or vegetables may be used (and when fruits or vegetables are used, Sri Lankans sometimes interchangeably use the words* sambol *and* sambola*).*

It is common for coconut sambol *to be toasted so that it may be kept for longer or even frozen, which works very well for its inclusion in rice bundles. To do this, quickly temper (see page 42) 2 Tbsp chopped red onion, 5 ripped curry leaves, and 1 tsp black mustard seeds together. Add the coconut* sambol *to the tempered mixture, quickly mixing and folding it with a spoon until all the moisture is removed and the coconut mixture is dry and nicely toasted.*

Serves 4–6

2 cups finely scraped coconut (either fresh, frozen, or desiccated, see page 34)

½ small red onion, peeled and finely chopped

2 tsp cayenne powder

2 Tbsp paprika

1 tsp dried Maldives fish, ground, or to taste (optional)

1 tsp fine sea salt, or to taste

2 Tbsp lime juice, or to taste

Onion Chili Sambol
Lunu Miris Sambol

A common relish-like accompaniment to milk rice, *lunu miris* translates literally as "onion chili" and gets its bite from the raw red onion, dried red chili, and the generous addition of salt. The addition of Maldives fish is common in Sri Lanka, but optional. Traditionally, all ingredients are ground together using a grinding stone to create a paste-like consistency. Alternatively, finely dicing the ingredients and then combining them in a bowl with a spoon also provides a pleasing and crunchy texture.

Serves 4–6

- 1 small red onion, chopped
- 1 Tbsp crushed dried chili pepper flakes or 1 tsp cayenne powder + 1 tsp paprika
- 1 tsp fine sea salt
- 1–2 Tbsp lime juice
- 1½ tsp dried Maldives fish (optional)

If you are using a mortar and pestle, pound all the ingredients together to almost a paste-like consistency.

If you are cutting by hand, finely chop the red onion. Put the onion into a bowl, add all the other ingredients, and combine with a spoon.

If you are using a chopper, pulse everything to achieve a very fine but not wet texture.

From spicy, to sweet and tangy, there are many recipe variations for onion-based sambols. These are the basic ingredients for three common preparations:

Lunu miris sambol *(onion chili): raw red onions mixed with dried red chili, salt, lime, with or without Maldives fish, all finely chopped or ground to a paste*

Lunu sambola *(onion salad): sliced raw white or red onions mixed with green chili, salt, and lime*

Seeni sambol *(sugar and onion tempered): sliced white or red onions that are tempered or fried and mixed with spices, sugar, and other condiments*

Pickles

In Sri Lanka, pickling is a common preparation for preserving fruits and vegetables, and even fish. The tartness, which is achieved by particular souring ingredients (see page 38) is balanced off with the sharpness of mustard seeds, pungency of onions, heat of chili, and the sweetness of sugar.

Eggplant Pickle
Wambatu Moju

Cut the eggplant into even pieces about 1-inch-long and ½-inch-wide.

Half-fill a medium-size pot with the 4 cups of oil. (You may not need all 4 cups.) Heat the oil on high until it is very hot but not smoking (350°–375°F). Fry the eggplant in small batches, taking care not to overcrowd the pot and gently turning the pieces until the flesh is golden brown, approximately 1 minute. Because the flesh is delicate, you have to keep a careful watch so the pieces don't burn.

Using a slotted spoon, remove the eggplant pieces from the pot and set them on a plate that has been covered with paper towels. Using another paper towel, gently pat the pieces to remove any excess oil. You should have about 1½ cups of fried eggplant.

In a frying pan over medium-high heat, warm the remaining 2 Tbsp of oil. When the oil is hot but not smoking, fry the onion just until translucent. Remove from the pan and set aside.

Add the chilies to the hot pan and fry until just lightly browned. Remove from the pan and set aside. Turn off the heat but keep the pan handy, as you'll use it again.

For the pickle marinade, mix together the garlic, ginger, sugar, cayenne, salt, vinegar, and mustard in a bowl.

Reheat the pan (add a little more oil if needed) over medium-high heat. When the oil is hot, add the fried eggplant, onion, chilies, and pickle marinade. Gently stir to combine all the ingredients and bring to a boil. Now turn off the heat but keep the pan on the stovetop and let the *moju* simmer, untouched, until cooled and slightly reduced.

Serves 4–6

FRYING

½ lb (1 medium-size) round Indian eggplant, stem removed

Approximately 4 cups + 2 Tbsp vegetable oil, divided

½ cup red pearl onion, previously soaked in water and skins removed

4 green (Thai) chilies

PICKLE MARINADE

2 garlic cloves, finely grated

1-inch piece fresh ginger, peeled and finely grated

1 tsp granulated sugar

1 tsp cayenne powder

½ tsp fine sea salt

⅓ cup white vinegar

3 Tbsp grainy mustard

Vegetable Pickle
Achcharu

Blanch all the vegetables and fruit separately in boiling salted water. Skin the onions. Set everything aside to cool.

In a large, non-reactive bowl (large enough to hold all the vegetables and fruit), mix together the ground mustard seeds, salt, sugar, cayenne, and vinegar. Add the vegetables and fruit and stir to coat.

Let sit until all the vegetables and fruit are at room temperature.

Spoon into a sterilized glass jar, seal, and refrigerate for 1 month before consuming. This may be kept in the fridge for up to 3 months.

Makes approximately 3½ cups

½ lb carrots, julienned

½ lb cauliflower, cut into small pieces

½ lb green papaya, julienned (optional)

¼ lb red pearl onions, skins removed

10 green (Thai) chilies

3 Tbsp black mustard seeds, ground

3 Tbsp fine sea salt

¼ tsp granulated sugar

Pinch of cayenne powder

1½ cups white vinegar

One medium-size (1 quart) sterilized Mason jar with lid

Salted Lime Preserve
Lunu Dehi

In Sri Lanka, salted limes are traditionally dried for several days in the sun, and then preserved in pickling liquid. In North America, my mother kept her salted lime preserve in a very large Mason jar, atop a high closed shelf in the kitchen. The limes would be unrecognizable from their former bright green state. After drying and sitting in seasoned lime juice, the limes turn brown and their flesh becomes chewy. It is all at once tart and tangy and a nice embellishment to rice and curries.

On day one, remove the pointed tail of the limes to create a flat base, so you can stand the limes up.

Using a sharp knife, slice crosswise and diagonally almost all the way down the centre of the limes (through the skin and right into the flesh), creating approximately eight wedges. Slightly pull the wedges apart almost to create the appearance of a blossoming flower. Place the limes in a square or rectangular glass dish (large and wide enough to hold all the limes).

Completely fill the gaps between the limes with the salt (about a tablespoon of salt per lime), but don't pour salt over top of the limes. Cover with plastic wrap and let sit for 48 hours.

On day three, remove the plastic wrap and check the skins for browning and that the juice of the limes is being released. Let sit, uncovered, on your worktop, where it will be undisturbed for 24 hours.

On day four, put the limes into a 200°F oven for 1 hour. Let stand, uncovered, at room temperature overnight. Do this for 7 days in a row.

After a week of this process, the limes should be completely dried with a brown colour and a dry texture.

For the brine, place the lime juice in a pot and add the curry powder, salt, and cayenne. Heat over medium-high heat for about 10 minutes. Let cool.

Place the limes in the sterilized jar. Pour the brine over the limes, seal the jar, and let sit for 4 weeks before consuming.

Makes about 4 cups

LIMES

5 large limes

Coarse kosher salt

BRINE

Juice of 10 large limes

2 heaping tsp roasted curry powder (page 31)

2 tsp fine sea salt

1 tsp cayenne powder

One medium-size (1 quart) sterilized Mason jar with lid

Small Bites with Tea

Fried Fish Cutlets
Malu Cutlis

Like many coastal communities, Sri Lanka has a local version of a savoury seafood cake or cutlet. My grandmother made fried fish cutlets using a local variety of fish called kingfish. This is a popular snack to serve company or to have with tea.

This recipe uses canned tuna, but one-half pound of fresh white fish such as halibut is nice so long as it is rinsed, skinned, and deboned.

In a large frying pan over medium-high heat, place 2 Tbsp of oil. Sauté the onion until it is translucent, but do not brown. Stir in the vinegar and then the chilies.

Add the tuna to the pan. Using the back of a fork, mash the tuna to break it into large chunks and then stir to combine the mixture. Add salt and pepper to taste.

Add the mashed potatoes gradually to the pan, mixing thoroughly and making sure all the ingredients are well combined. Taste and add more seasoning, as desired.

Squeeze the lime wedge over top, add the mint, stir to combine, and set aside to cool for about 20 minutes.

Once cooled, roll the mixture into small balls (roughly the size of small meatballs or doughnut holes), using the palms of your hands. Set aside on a plate.

For the batter, in a medium-size bowl and using a fork, mix the flour, a pinch of salt, ¼ cup of water, and egg into a smooth, lump-free batter. Set aside.

On a large plate, spread out the bread crumbs. Place the plate of fish balls next to the batter, and the batter next to the bread crumbs. Taking one at a time, coat the fish balls in batter and then crumbs. As you coat them, place them on plates until you're ready to cook them.

The cutlets can be deep-fried right away or can be frozen (in freezer-proof containers lined with foil and parchment paper) for up to 2 months.

Half-fill a medium-size pot with the oil. (You may not need all 4 cups.) Heat the oil on high until it is very hot but not smoking (350°F). Fry the cutlets in small batches, taking care not to overcrowd the pot, and gently turning the pieces until they are evenly browned. Do not overfry.

Using a slotted spoon, remove the cutlets from the pot and set them on a plate that has been covered with paper towels. Using another paper towel, gently pat the pieces to remove any excess oil. Serve right away or allow to cool slightly.

Serve with a spicy tomato sauce (see page 162) on the side.

Makes approximately 25 cutlets

BASIC FISH FILLING

2 Tbsp vegetable oil

1 medium-size white onion, finely chopped

1 Tbsp white vinegar

2 green (Thai) chilies, finely chopped

2 cans (each 170 grams) flaked white tuna, drained

1 tsp fine sea salt, or to taste

½ tsp ground black pepper, or to taste

2 large white potatoes, boiled and mashed

1 small lime wedge (yielding about 1 tsp juice)

1 tsp finely chopped mint

BATTER AND BREAD COATING

¼ cup all-purpose flour

Pinch of fine sea salt

1 egg, slightly beaten

2 cups fine dried bread crumbs

4 cups good-quality oil

Deep-Fried Stuffed Banana Peppers
Malu Miris

Sri Lanka is an island with a history of large families and extended family networks, and a big part of the culture is the gatherings, with a few small bites to aid in the merriment. Whether with afternoon tea, or served with drinks before a meal, sharing small bites is a way to relax and indulge in a few savoury treats.

Makes 6

6 medium capsicum/long yellow banana peppers

1 batch basic fish filling (page 161), cooled

1 batch bread coating (page 161)

4 cups good-quality oil

Bring a large pot of unsalted water to a boil. Blanch the banana peppers for about 2 minutes. Set the blanched peppers on a plate.

Trim the stems but do not cut them off completely. Slice each pepper vertically down the centre, but do not cut through it. Remove the seeds and white pith.

Stuff each pepper with fish filling, using your hands to press and work the mixture into the entire body to ensure it is filled.

Squeeze the two cut sides together to close each pepper. Swipe off any of the fish mixture that oozes out with the tip of your finger.

Bread the peppers (see page 161), making sure to double-coat them. This will help ensure an extra-crispy coating that won't crack when they're deep-fried. Use wider, deeper dishes to hold the wet batter and the bread crumbs as the peppers are long.

Half-fill a medium-size pot with the oil. (You may not need all 4 cups.) Heat the oil on high until it is very hot but not smoking (350°F). Fry the peppers in small batches, taking care not to overcrowd the pot and gently turning them until evenly browned.

Using a slotted spoon, remove the peppers from the pot and set them on a plate that has been covered with paper towels. Using another paper towel, gently pat the peppers to remove any excess oil. Serve with spicy tomato sauce (below).

Spicy Tomato Sauce

Makes 1 cup

1 cup ketchup

1½ tsp Worcestershire sauce

1–2 Tbsp soy sauce

1 tsp granulated white sugar

1 tsp preferred chili sauce or Tabasco sauce

Place all the ingredients in a small pot over medium-high heat. Bring to a boil, turn down the heat, and let simmer, uncovered, for 5 minutes. The colour should be maroon. Play with the soy sauce to obtain this colour. Serve the sauce warm.

Vegetable (Ribbon) Tea Sandwiches

Many Sri Lankans will recall these pretty, colourful sandwiches being served at children's birthday parties and with afternoon tea. They are made with thinly sliced white bread and boiled and smashed root vegetables, and sometimes a little finely sliced salad leaves. Beetroots and carrots might seem an unusual filling for a sandwich, but they are surprisingly tasty.

Each sandwich consists of three layers of filling—smashed beets, carrots, and finely sliced lettuce (if using)—and four slices of bread. Both sides of the bread are buttered, except for the outermost sides of the sandwich.

In separate bowls, smash the beets and the carrots until fairly smooth. Add salt and pepper to taste to each bowl, and mix to make two smooth spreads.

In another bowl, place the finely sliced lettuce (if using).

Begin by laying out slices of bread (four slices per sandwich), buttering all of the sides facing up. Spread one slice with a thin layer of mashed beets and top with a piece of bread, butter side down. Now butter the side facing up, spread it with mashed carrot, and top with another piece of bread, butter side down. Now butter the side facing up, spread the lettuce over it, and top with a piece of bread, butter side down.

Cut the crusts off the sandwich and cut into four triangles. Repeat for the desired number of sandwiches.

Yield: Flexible!

1 loaf thinly sliced white bread

2 medium-size beets, boiled and peeled, or 1 (400-gram) can of pickled beets, drained

2–3 carrots, boiled

Pinch of fine sea salt, or to taste

Pinch of ground black pepper, or to taste

½ head romaine or Boston lettuce, finely sliced (optional)

¼ cup butter, at room temperature

These are a wonderful way to use up extra or leftover root vegetables for a quick and easy lunch. You can also boil the veggies the night before and put them in the fridge for use the next day.

When I was taking my walks abroad one morning,

THE SEA COAST
about three million black-crabs-

Coffea travancorensis

Beverages

"A vast variety of mangoes, pineapples, green, yellow and red plantains, papaws, wood apples, mangosteens, rambutan, avocados, custard apples, cherimoyer, jambu, lovi-lovi, durian and jak, the largest fruit in the world, are some of the harvest fruits that in their luscious juicy sweetness are available in season."

(Doreen Alles, *Facets of Sri Lanka 2: Traditional Foods & Cookery Down the Ages*)

Fresh Papaya Juice
Papol Yusa

Papaya (or *papaw*) is one of the many fruits I grew to love as our family visited Sri Lanka over the years. The mere size these fruits can grow to is astounding. Papaya was one of several fruits my grandfather cultivated for a living. When my father picks up the fruit at the grocery store, he cups it in his hand, and says, "My father used to grow papaw half the length of my arm!" This refreshing juice is a wonderful start to the day.

For a sweet treat, use ginger ale in place of the water.

Cut the papayas in half. Scoop out the seeds with a spoon and discard them. Scoop out the flesh of the papayas and drop it into a blender.

Add 1 cup of water, lemon juice, sugar, and salt to the blender. Blend until smooth. Taste, and add more water and/or sweetener to your liking. Serve chilled.

Makes 4 servings

6 small overripe papayas

½ cup lemon juice (approximately from 2 large lemons)

½ cup granulated sugar, or more to taste

½ tsp fine sea salt

You may use bottled lemon juice in place of the fresh.

Fresh Passion Juice
Vel dodan Yusa

The exotic flavour of passion fruit is delicately sweet with a trace of floral notes. While in Sri Lanka the yellow variety is used for drinks, in North America you may find the purple variety more available at the grocery store in the summer. This is lovely served as a breakfast beverage.

❧

Cut each passion fruit in half. Scoop out the flesh and seeds and drop them all into a blender.

Add 4 cups of water, lemon juice, sugar, and salt to the blender. Blend until smooth.

Strain the juice through a fine-mesh sieve into a jug. Discard the ground seeds. Taste, and add more water and/or sugar to your liking. Serve chilled.

Makes 4 servings

10 ripe passion fruits (yellow if they are available, otherwise purple)

¼ cup fresh lemon juice (from 1–2 large lemons)

½ cup granulated sugar, or to taste

½ tsp fine sea salt

You may use 3–4 Tbsp of bottled lemon juice in place of the fresh.

Fresh Lime Juice
Dehi Yusa

In Sri Lanka, limes have long been used for their acidic, medicinal, and purifying qualities. Lime juice is particularly energizing in hot weather and is my favourite fresh juice drink when I'm visiting Sri Lanka. I love its tart, refreshing flavour. Lime varieties found in Sri Lanka are typically very small, which makes them easy to use and cook with. For this recipe you may use medium-size limes.

❧

Place the lime juice in a serving jug. Add 3 cups of water, the sugar, and the salt. Stir well. Serve chilled.

Makes 4 servings

1 cup fresh lime juice (8 small to medium-size limes)

7 Tbsp granulated sugar

½ tsp fine salt

Milk Tea for Two Poured at a Height
Kiri Thē

Kandy's hill country is the heart of the island's tea cultivation region, where the world's best tea is grown. Tea is the first thing that hits a Sri Lankan's stomach in the morning, and one tends to consume cup after filled-to-the-brim cup throughout the day. There are no hard and fast rules on how to drink tea: plain black, strong or light, with a lot or a little milk, with sugar, condensed milk, or a bit of *jaggery* (unrefined palm tree sugar). But locals often prefer to drink it with nicely warmed milk and as sweet as dessert. Pouring tea at a height is actually a practised skill whereby hot milk tea (tea with milk that has been separately warmed) is quickly poured back and forth between two vessels. This method is said to make for a more satisfying frothy cup of tea.

My mother used to prepare tea for me this way (though in less overstated form) in the evenings at home, and on cold winter days it was most comforting!

You can adjust the strength of the tea to you and your guests' preference by adding more or fewer leaves.

Pour a little of some just-boiled water into 2 teacups and your teapot. Swirl it around and then discard.

Place the tea bags (or tea leaves) in the teapot, pour in 2½ cups of just-boiled filtered water, and let steep for 3 to 4 minutes.

While the tea is steeping, heat the milk to a very warm but not overly hot temperature.

Remove tea bags if using, and pour or strain the tea into one of the jugs. Add the warmed milk and the sugar. Stir well.

Holding the jug with the milk tea in one hand at a height—as high as you are comfortable—quickly pour it into the other vessel, held below. Quickly pour the tea back and forth between the vessels in this manner several times. This will create a light froth in the tea.

Pour the foamy hot milk tea into the teacups, and add a vanilla bean (if using) to each cup as a stir stick/garnish.

Serves 2

2½ cups just-boiled filtered water

2 tea bags of black Ceylon tea or 1½–2 tsp high-quality loose black Ceylon tea leaves

½ cup cow's milk (preferably full fat)

2 tsp granulated sugar

2 vanilla beans, each neatly slit down the middle but not split or broken (optional)

2 pouring vessels (glass or metal measuring jugs will work)

Ginger Tea for Two
Inguru Thē

The warm spiciness of ginger tea is comforting on chilly days or during the winter season. If you prefer a stronger cup of ginger tea, you may grate or crush the ginger pieces. You may also keep a couple of slices in the tea after you have strained the tea bag/leaves.

Pour some just-boiled water into 2 teacups and your teapot. Swirl it around and then discard.

Place the tea bags (or tea leaves) and ginger in the teapot, pour in 2½ cups just-boiled filtered water, and let steep for 3 to 4 minutes.

Remove tea bags if using, and pour or strain the tea into the teacups, and add sugar (or honey) to taste.

Makes 2 cups

2 tea bags of black Ceylon tea or 1½–2 tsp high-quality loose black Ceylon tea leaves

1-inch piece fresh ginger sliced or finely grated

Sugar or honey (optional)

Iced Coffee
Iced Coppee

Iced coffee is a favoured Sri Lankan treat. This recipe is slightly creamy and sweet, and it's a lovely beverage to serve at parties with a spread of savoury small bites. The recipe may easily be doubled for larger crowds.

In a large pot over high heat, place the milk and sugar. Bring the milk to a boil, stirring frequently, until the sugar completely dissolves. When the milk starts to bubble up, remove the pot from the heat.

Add the coffee to the hot milk, stir to combine, and adjust the sugar to taste. Set aside to cool.

Once the coffee has cooled completely, add the brandy (if using) and vanilla, and stir to combine. Refrigerate for a few hours, and serve with an ice cube for an extra chilly drink.

Serves 4–6

2 cups full-fat cow's milk

¼ cup granulated sugar, or to taste

3 cups hot strong coffee

2 Tbsp brandy (optional)

1 tsp pure vanilla extract

Acknowledgements

My publisher, Taryn Boyd, for sharing in my dream and giving a beautiful and deserved home for this book. My editor, Lesley Cameron, for your care and perspective. Photographer Danielle Acken, food stylist Aurelia Louvet, and assistant Naomi Singh for bringing life and exacting light and depth to the details. Designer Tree Abraham for seeing the vision and constructing an artwork. Kate Kennedy, for your bird's-eye view and coordinating the many elements.

My friends Jo-anne Lauzer and Natasha Asseltine, I am ever grateful for our serendipitous reunion and your contributions that illuminated this work.

My mother and father, without whom this book would not be possible. Amma, I thank you for all the years in the kitchen, and the countless hours hovering over pots and pans on stove tops. For taking the unusual and unfamiliar step of measuring spices. All the patience only a mother could have, and all the stories and secrets only a mother would share.

My sister, my family, and friends who have supported and shared my passion for Sri Lankan cookery.

Finally, my husband, the love of my life, all of my heart for your unconditional support, encouragement, steadfast belief, and tireless taste testing! My dear daughter, the laughter in my heart, all of this is for you.

178

Photo Captions

The following photos are from the author's personal collection

Back cover (top) The author's grandmother and mother in Kandy, Sri Lanka; (bottom) The author's father, Sri Lanka

p. 8 (top left) The author's mother and a young child, Peradeniya, Kandy; (top right) Avocados, roadside stall, Central Province, Sri Lanka

p. 10 (left) Paddy (rice) fields, Central Province, Sri Lanka; (right) Lotus flower, Sri Lanka

p. 11 The author's mother, grandmother, and cousin at the family home, Peradeniya, Kandy

p. 13 Orchid at Royal Botanical Gardens, Peradeniya, Kandy

p. 14 (top right) Banana peppers, Kandy Central Market

p. 17 (top) The author's mother with her brother, family, and friends on a bridge, Kandy; (bottom) Banana flower, Kandy Central Market

p. 20 (top) Coconut, Sri Lanka

p. 23 (top) The author's mother with three of her brothers and her mother, family friends, and the domestic staff, at the family home in Peradeniya, Kandy; (middle) Hoppers (aapa), string hoppers (idiappan), coconut sambol, and pittu; (bottom) The author's aunt at her house in Peradeniya, Kandy

p. 28 (top) Two young boys, Peradeniya, Kandy; (bottom) Green (un-ripened) pepper plant

p. 32 The author's mother with her friends at the family home in Peradeniya, Kandy

p. 38 (left) The author's mother and a family friend at the family home in Peradeniya, Kandy; (right) Durian fruits, Kandy Central Market

p. 39 Bananas, Kandy Central Market

p. 44 (left) Statue of Buddha, temple, Sri Lanka; (right) Green palm leaf

p. 46 (top) The author's mother with friends, Peradeniya, Kandy

p. 48 (top) The author's grandmother and mother, Kandy; (bottom) Man sun-drying peppercorns at the family home, Peradeniya, Kandy

p. 54 Vegetables being weighed on a scale, Kandy Central Market

p. 62 The author's grandmother at a temple, Sri Lanka

p. 68 Beetroots, Kandy Central Market

p. 76 A vendor with produce for sale, Kandy Central Market

p. 82 Okra, Kandy Central Market

p. 84 Green beans being weighed on a scale, Kandy Central Market

p. 96 Green (un-ripened) mangoes on a tree, Sri Lanka

p. 97 Tomatoes, Kandy Central Market

p. 102 Pulses, dried red chilies, red onions, potatoes, Kandy Central Market

p. 108 A family friend with the author's cousin, Peradeniya, Kandy

p. 122 (bottom) The author's father, Sri Lanka

p. 130 Crab curry, Sri Lanka

p. 139 Fruits (papaw, star fruit, pineapple, rambutan, mango, and baby bananas) at the home of the author's grandmother, Peradeniya, Kandy

p. 142 Eggplants, Kandy Central Market

p. 146 Pineapples, Sri Lanka

p. 176 (clockwise from top left) Palm trees, Sri Lanka; The author's uncle and aunt in Peradeniya; The author's grandmother and mother, Sri Lanka; The author's father, Ontario, Canada

p. 177 (top) Rice (paddy) fields, Central Province, Sri Lanka; (bottom) The author's mother, grandmother, and family friend

p. 178 The author's mother with friends at the family home, Peradeniya, Kandy

Index

A
Achcharu, 155
Ala Badthum, 67
Ala Maluwa, 66
Alu Kesel Gedi Badthum, 95
Ambul Thiyal, 129
Amu Amba Curry, 96
Amu Papol Mallum, 151
Amu Thuna Paha Kudu, 31
Annasi Maluwa, 93
Annasi Salada, 147
Asian markets, 34

B
Badthupa Moong Ata, 105
Badupa Thuna Paha Kudu, 31
banana leaves
    about, 39–40
    Batmula, 61
    Rice and Curries Packed in Banana Leaves (Batmula), 61
banana peppers. *see* peppers, banana
Bandakka (Badthala) Curry, 83
Batmula, 61
beans
    Green Bean White Curry (Bonchi Suthu Curry), 85
    Mung Bean Curry (Mung Ata Maluwa), 104
    Roasted Mung Bean Curry (Badthupa Moong Ata), 105
    Tempered Snake Beans (Makaral Thel Dala), 87
beef
    Beef Curry (Harak Mas Curry), 115
    Peppered Beef with Coconut Milk and Mustard Seed (Harak Mas Gam Miris Pol Kiri Badthum), 117
    Rice and Curries Packed in Banana Leaves (Batmula), 61
beetroots
    Beetroot Curry (Rathu Ala Maluwa), 71
    Fried Beetroots (Rathu Ala Badthum), 69
    Vegetable (Ribbon) Tea Sandwiches, 163
Biththara Kiri Hothi, 113
black curry, about, 30
black mustard seeds. *see* mustard seeds
Bonchi Suthu Curry, 85
British culinary influence, 47

C
Cabbage Curry (Gova Maluwa), 77
cardamom (enasal)
    about, 24
    Cashew Nut Curry (Kadju Maluwa), 99
    Tomato Curry (Thakkali Maluwa), 97
    Young Jackfruit Curry (Polos Ambula), 91
carrots
    Carrot Curry (Carrot Maluwa), 74
    Carrot Slaw (Carrot Sambola), 138
    Vegetable (Ribbon) Tea Sandwiches, 163
    Vegetable Pickle (Achcharu), 155
cashews
    Cashew Nut Curry (Kadju Maluwa), 99
    Fancy Yellow Rice (Kaha Bath), 53–55
cauliflower
    Cauliflower, Potatoes, and Green Peas Curry (Malgova, Ala, Peas Ata Maluwa), 79
    Vegetable Pickle (Achcharu), 155
chicken
    Chicken Curry (Kukul Mas Curry), 111
    Ghee Rice (Elagi Thel Bath), 57
chili flakes
    Chili Pepper Dal (Parippu Mirisata), 103
    Devilled Potatoes (Ala Badthum), 67
    Devilled Prawns (Isso Badthum), 125
    Onion Chili Sambol (Lunu Miris Sambol), 153
    Prawn Curry (Isso Curry), 126
    Tempered Leeks (Leeks Thel Dala), 75
chili peppers (miris). *see also* chili flakes; chilies, green
    about, 24

Eggplant Curry (Wambatu/Badthala Curry), 81
chilies, green
    as a key ingredient, 35
    Beef Curry (Harak Mas Curry), 115
    Beetroot Curry (Rathu Ala Maluwa), 71
    Bitter Gourd Salad (Karavila/Badthala Sambola), 141
    Boiled Eggs with Coconut Milk (Biththara Kiri Hothi), 113
    Cabbage Curry (Gova Maluwa), 77
    Carrot Curry (Carrot Maluwa), 74
    Carrot Slaw (Carrot Sambola), 138
    Cauliflower, Potatoes, and Green Peas Curry (Malgova, Ala, Peas Ata Maluwa), 79
    Chicken Curry (Kukul Mas Curry), 111
    Crab Curry (Kakuluwo Curry), 131
    Cucumber Salad (Pipinna Sambola), 135
    Eggplant Pickle (Wambatu Moju), 154
    Eggplant Salad (Wambatu/Badthala Sambola), 143
    Fried Fish Cutlets (Malu Cutlis), 161
    Fried Plantain Curry (Alu Kesel Gedi Badthum), 95
    Green Bean White Curry (Bonchi Suthu Curry), 85
    Kale Mallum, 150
    Okra Curry (Bandakka/Badthala Curry), 83
    Parsley Salad (Parsley Sambola), 145
    Pineapple Curry (Annasi Maluwa), 93
    Raw Papaya Mallum (Amu Papol Mallum), 151
    Sour Fish Curry (Ambul Thiyal), 129
    Vegetable Pickle (Achcharu), 155
    White Fish Curry (Suthu Malu Curry), 127
    White Potato Curry (Suthu Ala Curry), 65
    Winter Squash Curry (Wattakka Curry), 73
    Yellow Dal with/without Spinach (Parippu/Nivithi Parippu), 101
chopping, food, 34, 39
cinnamon (kurundu)
    about, 24
    Fancy Yellow Rice (Kaha Bath), 53–55
    Roasted Curry Powder (Badupa Thuna Paha Kudu), 31
    Unroasted Curry Powder- Raw (Amu Thuna Paha Kudu), 31
cloves (karabu nati)
    about, 24–25

Beef Curry (Harak Mas Curry), 115
Chicken Curry (Kukul Mas Curry), 111
Tomato Curry (Thakkali Maluwa), 97
Young Jackfruit Curry (Polos Ambula), 91
coconut (pol). *see also* coconut milk (pol kiri)
    about, 21
    buying, 34, 42
    Black Pork Curry (Kalu Uru Mas Curry), 119
    Carrot Slaw (Carrot Sambola), 138
    Coconut Roti (Pol Roti), 59
    Coconut Sambol (Pol Sambol), 152
    Kale Mallum, 150
    Parsley Salad (Parsley Sambola), 145
    Raw Papaya Mallum (Amu Papol Mallum), 151
    Rice and Curries Packed in Banana Leaves (Batmula), 61
coconut milk (pol kiri)
    about, 21
    Beef Curry (Harak Mas Curry), 115
    Beetroot Curry (Rathu Ala Maluwa), 71
    Boiled Eggs with Coconut Milk (Biththara Kiri Hothi), 113
    Cabbage Curry (Gova Maluwa), 77
    Carrot Curry (Carrot Maluwa), 74
    Cashew Nut Curry (Kadju Maluwa), 99
    Cauliflower, Potatoes, and Green Peas Curry (Malgova, Ala, Peas Ata Maluwa), 79
    Chicken Curry (Kukul Mas Curry), 111
    Crab Curry (Kakuluwo Curry), 131
    Cucumber Salad Village-Style (Gama Pipinna Sambola), 138
    Eggplant Curry (Wambatu/Badthala Curry), 81
    Fried Plantain Curry (Alu Kesel Gedi Badthum), 95
    Green Bean White Curry (Bonchi Suthu Curry), 85
    Mango Curry (Amu Amba Curry), 96
    Milk Rice (Kiri Bath), 51
    Mung Bean Curry (Mung Ata Maluwa), 104
    Okra Curry (Bandakka/Badthala Curry), 83
    Peppered Beef with Coconut Milk and Mustard Seed (Harak Mas Gam Miris Pol Kiri Badthum), 117
    Pineapple Curry (Annasi Maluwa), 93
    Prawn Curry (Isso Curry), 126
    Red Potato Curry (Ala Maluwa), 66
    Roasted Mung Bean Curry (Badthupa Moong

coconut milk (*continued*)
    Ata), 105
    Tomato Curry (Thakkali Maluwa), 97
    White Fish Curry (Suthu Malu Curry), 127
    White Potato Curry (Suthu Ala Curry), 65
    Winter Squash Curry (Wattakka Curry), 73
    Yellow Dal with/without Spinach (Parippu/Nivithi Parippu), 101
    Young Jackfruit Curry (Polos Ambula), 91
coconut shell spoons, 33
coffee. *see* drinks
cooking methods, 15, 42–43
cooking utensils, 33
cookware, 33
coriander seeds (kothamalli)
    about, 25
    Roasted Curry Powder (Badupa Thuna Paha Kudu), 31
    Unroasted Curry Powder- Raw (Amu Thuna Paha Kudu), 31
Crab Curry (Kakuluwo Curry), 131
cucumber
    Cucumber Salad (Pipinna Sambola), 135
    Cucumber Salad Village-Style (Gama Pipinna Sambola), 138
    Pineapple Salad (Annasi Salada), 147
    Tomato, Cucumber, and Red Onion Salad (Thakkali, Pipinna, Rathu Lunu Salada), 137
curry. *see also* curry leaves (karapincha); curry powder; curry, meat; curry, seafood and fish
    about, 30
    black curry, about, 30
    red curry, about, 30
    texture and consistency, 43–45
    Beetroot Curry (Rathu Ala Maluwa), 71
    Carrot Curry (Carrot Maluwa), 74
    Cashew Nut Curry (Kadju Maluwa), 99
    Cauliflower, Potatoes, and Green Peas Curry (Malgova, Ala, Peas Ata Maluwa), 79
    Eggplant Curry (Wambatu/Badthala Curry), 81
    Fried Plantain Curry (Alu Kesel Gedi Badthum), 95
    Green Bean White Curry (Bonchi Suthu Curry), 85
    Mango Curry (Amu Amba Curry), 96
    Mung Bean Curry (Mung Ata Maluwa), 104
    Okra Curry (Bandakka/Badthala Curry), 83
    Pineapple Curry (Annasi Maluwa), 93
    Rice and Curries Packed in Banana Leaves (Batmula), 61
    Tomato Curry (Thakkali Maluwa), 97
    White Potato Curry (Suthu Ala Curry), 65
    Winter Squash Curry (Wattakka Curry), 73
    Young Jackfruit Curry (Polos Ambula), 91
curry leaves (karapincha)
    about, 25
    as a key ingredient, 35
    using, 40
curry powder
    roasting, 30
    Roasted Curry Powder (Badupa Thuna Paha Kudu), 31
    Unroasted Curry Powder- Raw (Amu Thuna Paha Kudu), 31
curry, meat
    Beef Curry (Harak Mas Curry), 115
    Black Pork Curry (Kalu Uru Mas Curry), 119
    Chicken Curry (Kukul Mas Curry), 111
curry, seafood and fish
    Crab Curry (Kakuluwo Curry), 131
    Prawn Curry (Isso Curry), 126
    Sour Fish Curry (Ambul Thiyal), 129
    White Fish Curry (Suthu Malu Curry), 127

D

dal curry (parippu)
    about consistency, 45
    Chili Pepper Dal (Parippu Mirisata), 103
    Yellow Dal with/without Spinach (Parippu/Nivithi Parippu), 101
Dehi Yusa, 169
dressing
    Eggplant Salad (Wambatu/Badthala Sambola), 143
    Pineapple Salad (Annasi Salada), 147
    Tomato, Cucumber, and Red Onion Salad (Thakkali, Pipinna, Rathu Lunu Salada), 137
drinks
    Fresh Lime Juice (Dehi Yusa), 169
    Fresh Papaya Juice (Papol Yusa), 167

Fresh Passion Juice (Vel dodan Yusa), 169
Ginger Tea for Two (Inguru Thē), 172
Iced Coffee (Iced Coppee), 173
Milk Tea for Two Poured at a Height (Kiri Thē), 171
Dutch culinary influence, 47

E
eggplant
Eggplant Curry (Wambatu/Badthala Curry), 81
Eggplant Pickle (Wambatu Moju), 154
Eggplant Salad (Wambatu/Badthala Sambola), 143
Rice and Curries Packed in Banana Leaves (Batmula), 61
eggs
Boiled Eggs with Coconut Milk (Biththara Kiri Hothi), 113
Fancy Yellow Rice (Kaha Bath), 53–55
Elagi Thel Bath, 57
electric food choppers, 33–34

F
farmers' markets, 34
fennel seeds (maduru)
about, 25
Roasted Curry Powder (Badupa Thuna Paha Kudu), 31
Unroasted Curry Powder- Raw (Amu Thuna Paha Kudu), 31
fenugreek seeds (uluhaal)
about, 25
Ala Maluwa, 66
Beetroot Curry (Rathu Ala Maluwa), 71
Boiled Eggs with Coconut Milk (Biththara Kiri Hothi), 113
Cabbage Curry (Gova Maluwa), 77
Cauliflower, Potatoes, and Green Peas Curry (Malgova, Ala, Peas Ata Maluwa), 79
Crab Curry (Kakuluwo Curry), 131
Fried Plantain Curry (Alu Kesel Gedi Badthum), 95
Mango Curry (Amu Amba Curry), 96
Okra Curry (Bandakka/Badthala Curry), 83
Pineapple Curry (Annasi Maluwa), 93
Red Potato Curry (Ala Maluwa), 66
Tempered Snake Beans (Makaral Thel Dala), 87
White Fish Curry (Suthu Malu Curry), 127
White Potato Curry (Suthu Ala Curry), 65
Winter Squash Curry (Wattakka Curry), 73
fish. *see also* Maldives fish (umbalakada)
Coconut Sambol (Pol Sambol), 152
Deep-Fried Stuffed Banana Peppers (Malu Miris), 162
Fried Fish Cutlets (Malu Cutlis), 161
Onion Chili Sambol (Lunu Miris Sambol), 153
Red Potato Curry (Ala Maluwa), 66
Rice and Curries Packed in Banana Leaves (Batmula), 61
Sour Fish Curry (Ambul Thiyal), 129
Tempered Snake Beans (Makaral Thel Dala), 87
White Fish Curry (Suthu Malu Curry), 127
food choppers, electric, 33–34

G
Gama Pipinna Sambola, 138
garcinia cambogia. *see* goraka (garcinia cambogia)
garlic
as a key ingredient, 35
Black Pork Curry (Kalu Uru Mas Curry), 119
Crab Curry (Kakuluwo Curry), 131
Devilled Prawns (Isso Badthum), 125
Eggplant Curry (Wambatu/Badthala Curry), 81
Fried Pork with Onions and Banana Peppers (Uru Mas Badthum), 121
Peppered Beef with Coconut Milk and Mustard Seed (Harak Mas Gam Miris Pol Kiri Badthum), 117
Prawn Curry (Isso Curry), 126
Tempered Leeks (Leeks Thel Dala), 75
Tomato Curry (Thakkali Maluwa), 97
Winter Squash Curry (Wattakka Curry), 73
ghee
Fancy Yellow Rice (Kaha Bath), 53–55
Ghee Rice (Elagi Thel Bath), 57
ginger (inguru)
about, 25, 35
Beef Curry (Harak Mas Curry), 115
Black Pork Curry (Kalu Uru Mas Curry), 119
Chicken Curry (Kukul Mas Curry), 111
Crab Curry (Kakuluwo Curry), 131

ginger (*continued*)
    Cucumber Salad Village-Style (Gama Pipinna Sambola), 138
    Devilled Prawns (Isso Badthum), 125
    Eggplant Curry (Wambatu/Badthala Curry), 81
    Fried Pork with Onions and Banana Peppers (Uru Mas Badthum), 121
    Ginger Tea for Two (Inguru Thē), 172
    Peppered Beef with Coconut Milk and Mustard Seed (Harak Mas Gam Miris Pol Kiri Badthum), 117
    Prawn Curry (Isso Curry), 126
    Sour Fish Curry (Ambul Thiyal), 129
goraka (garcinia cambogia)
    about, 25
    Black Pork Curry (Kalu Uru Mas Curry), 119
    Sour Fish Curry (Ambul Thiyal), 129
    Young Jackfruit Curry (Polos Ambula), 91
Gourd Salad (Karavila/Badthala Sambola), Bitter, 141
Gova Maluwa, 77

H
halibut
    Sour Fish Curry (Ambul Thiyal), 129
    White Fish Curry (Suthu Malu Curry), 127
Harak Mas Curry, 115
Harak Mas Gam Miris Pol Kiri Badthum, 117

I
Inguru Thē, 172
Isso Badthum, 125
Isso Curry, 126

J
jackfruit
    about, 42
    cooking methods, 15, 42
    Young Jackfruit Curry (Polos Ambula), 91

K
Kadju Maluwa, 99
Kaha Bath, 53–55
kakulu hal (short-grain red rice), 51
Kakuluwo Curry, 131
Kale Mallum, 150
Kalu Uru Mas Curry, 119
Karavila (Badthala) Sambola, 141
Kiri Bath, 51
Kiri Thē, 171
knives, 34
Kukul Mas Curry, 111

L
Leeks (Leeks Thel Dala), Tempered, 75
Leeks Thel Dala, 75
lemon grass (sera)
    about, 25
    Beef Curry (Harak Mas Curry), 115
    Ghee Rice (Elagi Thel Bath), 57
    Prawn Curry (Isso Curry), 126
lentils
    about, 42
    Chili Pepper Dal (Parippu Mirisata), 103
    Yellow Dal with/without Spinach (Parippu/Nivithi Parippu), 101
lettuce
    Tomato, Cucumber, and Red Onion Salad (Thakkali, Pipinna, Rathu Lunu Salada), 137
    Vegetable (Ribbon) Tea Sandwiches, 163
lime juice
    about, 38
    Fresh Lime Juice (Dehi Yusa), 169
Lime Preserve (Lunu Dehi), Salted, 157
Lunu Dehi, 157
Lunu Miris Sambol, 153
Lunu Sambola, 153

M
Makaral Thel Dala, 87
Maldives fish (umbalakada)
    about, 29
    Coconut Sambol (Pol Sambol), 152
    Mallum, 150
    Onion Chili Sambol (Lunu Miris Sambol), 153
    Red Potato Curry (Ala Maluwa), 66
    Tempered Snake Beans (Makaral Thel Dala), 87

Malgova, Ala, Peas Ata Maluwa, 79
mallum
    about, 45
    Kale Mallum, 150
    Raw Papaya Mallum (Amu Papol Mallum), 151
Malu Cutlis, 161
Malu Miris, 162
mangoes
    cutting, 41
    Mango Curry (Amu Amba Curry), 96
meats, slow-cooking methods, 42
Milk Tea for Two Poured at a Height (Kiri Thē), 171
mint
    Fancy Yellow Rice (Kaha Bath), 53–55
    Fried Fish Cutlets (Malu Cutlis), 161
    Pineapple Salad (Annasi Salada), 147
miris gala, 15
mol gaha, 15
moringa leaves
    Crab Curry (Kakuluwo Curry), 131
Mung Ata Maluwa, 104
mung beans
    Mung Bean Curry (Mung Ata Maluwa), 104
    Roasted Mung Bean Curry (Badthupa Moong Ata), 105
mustard (aba). *see also* mustard seeds
    about, 29–30, 42
    Eggplant Curry (Wambatu/Badthala Curry), 81
    Peppered Beef with Coconut Milk and Mustard Seed (Harak Mas Gam Miris Pol Kiri Badthum), 117
    Raw Papaya Mallum (Amu Papol Mallum), 151
mustard seeds
    about, 29–30, 42, 43
    Cabbage Curry (Gova Maluwa), 77
    Carrot Curry (Carrot Maluwa), 74
    Cucumber Salad Village-Style (Gama Pipinna Sambola), 138
    Mango Curry (Amu Amba Curry), 96
    Pineapple Curry (Annasi Maluwa), 93
    Red Potato Curry (Ala Maluwa), 66
    Vegetable Pickle (Achcharu), 155
    Winter Squash Curry (Wattakka Curry), 73

O

Okra Curry (Bandakka/Badthala Curry), 83
onions. *see also* onions, red
    as a key ingredient, 35
    Beetroot Curry (Rathu Ala Maluwa), 71
    Cabbage Curry (Gova Maluwa), 77
    Carrot Curry (Carrot Maluwa), 74
    Cucumber Salad (Pipinna Sambola), 135
    Eggplant Pickle (Wambatu Moju), 154
    Fancy Yellow Rice (Kaha Bath), 53–55
    Fried Beetroots (Rathu Ala Badthum), 69
    Fried Fish Cutlets (Malu Cutlis), 161
    Fried Pork with Onions and Banana Peppers (Uru Mas Badthum), 121
    Ghee Rice (Elagi Thel Bath), 57
    Lunu Sambola, 153
    Onion Chili Sambol, 153
    Peppered Beef with Coconut Milk and Mustard Seed (Harak Mas Gam Miris Pol Kiri Badthum), 117
    Prawn Curry (Isso Curry), 126
    Red Potato Curry (Ala Maluwa), 66
    Seeni Sambol, 153
    Vegetable Pickle (Achcharu), 155
    White Potato Curry (Suthu Ala Curry), 65
    Winter Squash Curry (Wattakka Curry), 73
    Yellow Dal with/without Spinach (Parippu/Nivithi Parippu), 101
onions, red
    Beef Curry (Harak Mas Curry), 115
    Bitter Gourd Salad (Karavila/Badthala Sambola), 141
    Black Pork Curry (Kalu Uru Mas Curry), 119
    Boiled Eggs with Coconut Milk (Biththara Kiri Hothi), 113
    Carrot Slaw (Carrot Sambola), 138
    Cashew Nut Curry (Kadju Maluwa), 99
    Cauliflower, Potatoes, and Green Peas Curry (Malgova, Ala, Peas Ata Maluwa), 79
    Chicken Curry (Kukul Mas Curry), 111
    Chili Pepper Dal (Parippu Mirisata), 103
    Coconut Sambol (Pol Sambol), 152
    Crab Curry (Kakuluwo Curry), 131
    Eggplant Curry (Wambatu/Badthala Curry), 81
    Eggplant Salad (Wambatu/Badthala Sambola), 143
    Fried Plantain Curry (Alu Kesel Gedi

onions, red (*continued*)
    Badthum), 95
  Green Bean White Curry (Bonchi Suthu Curry), 85
  Kale Mallum, 150
  Mango Curry (Amu Amba Curry), 96
  Mung Bean Curry (Mung Ata Maluwa), 104
  Okra Curry (Bandakka/Badthala Curry), 83
  Onion Chili Sambol (Lunu Miris Sambol), 153
  Parsley Salad (Parsley Sambola), 145
  Pineapple Curry (Annasi Maluwa), 93
  Pineapple Salad (Annasi Salada), 147
  Raw Papaya Mallum (Amu Papol Mallum), 151
  Roasted Mung Bean Curry (Badthupa Moong Ata), 105
  Sour Fish Curry (Ambul Thiyal), 129
  Tempered Snake Beans (Makaral Thel Dala), 87
  Tomato Curry (Thakkali Maluwa), 97
  Tomato, Cucumber, and Red Onion Salad (Thakkali, Pipinna, Rathu Lunu Salada), 137
  White Fish Curry (Suthu Malu Curry), 127
  Young Jackfruit Curry (Polos Ambula), 91

P

pan-frying, about, 43
pandan/pandanus leaf
  about, 29
  Beef Curry (Harak Mas Curry), 115
  Boiled Eggs with Coconut Milk (Biththara Kiri Hothi), 113
  Cashew Nut Curry (Kadju Maluwa), 99
  Cauliflower, Potatoes, and Green Peas Curry (Malgova, Ala, Peas Ata Maluwa), 79
  Chicken Curry (Kukul Mas Curry), 111
  Chili Pepper Dal (Parippu Mirisata), 103
  Fancy Yellow Rice (Kaha Bath), 53–55
  Fried Plantain Curry (Alu Kesel Gedi Badthum), 95
  Fried Pork with Onions and Banana Peppers (Uru Mas Badthum), 121
  Ghee Rice (Elagi Thel Bath), 57
  Mango Curry (Amu Amba Curry), 96
  Prawn Curry (Isso Curry), 126
  Roasted Mung Bean Curry (Badthupa Moong Ata), 105
  Sour Fish Curry (Ambul Thiyal), 129
  White Potato Curry (Suthu Ala Curry), 65
  Young Jackfruit Curry (Polos Ambula), 91
papaya
  Coconut Sambol (Pol Sambol), 152
  Fresh Papaya Juice (Papol Yusa), 167
  Raw Papaya Mallum (Amu Papol Mallum), 151
  Vegetable Pickle (Achcharu), 155
Papol Yusa, 167
Parippu Mirisata, 103
Parippu/Nivithi Parippu, 101
Parsley Sambola, 145
passion fruit
  Fresh Passion Juice (Vel dodan Yusa), 169
Peas Curry (Malgova, Ala, Peas Ata Maluwa), Cauliflower, Potatoes, and Green, 79
pennywort
  Parsley Salad (Parsley Sambola), 145
pepper (gammiris), about, 29
peppers. *see also* peppers, banana
  Devilled Prawns (Isso Badthum), 125
  Eggplant Salad (Wambatu/Badthala Sambola), 143
  Pineapple Salad (Annasi Salada), 147
peppers, banana
  Deep-Fried Stuffed Banana Peppers (Malu Miris), 162
  Devilled Prawns (Isso Badthum), 125
  Fried Beetroots (Rathu Ala Badthum), 69
  Fried Pork with Onions and Banana Peppers (Uru Mas Badthum), 121
  Peppered Beef with Coconut Milk and Mustard Seed (Harak Mas Gam Miris Pol Kiri Badthum), 117
pickles
  Eggplant Pickle (Wambatu Moju), 154
  Vegetable Pickle (Achcharu), 155
pineapples
  cutting, 41
  Pineapple Curry (Annasi Maluwa), 93
  Pineapple Salad (Annasi Salada), 147
Pipinna Sambola, 135
Plantain Curry (Alu Kesel Gedi Badthum), Fried, 95
Pol Sambol, 152
Polos Ambula, 91
pork

Black Pork Curry (Kalu Uru Mas Curry), 119
Fried Pork with Onions and Banana Peppers (Uru Mas Badthum), 121
Portuguese culinary influence, 47
potatoes
    Cauliflower, Potatoes, and Green Peas Curry (Malgova, Ala, Peas Ata Maluwa), 79
    Devilled Potatoes (Ala Badthum), 67
    Fried Fish Cutlets (Malu Cutlis), 161
    Red Potato Curry (Ala Maluwa), 66
    White Potato Curry (Suthu Ala Curry), 65
pots and pans, 33
prawns
    Devilled Prawns (Isso Badthum), 125
    Prawn Curry (Isso Curry), 126
preparation, food, 34, 39
Preserve (Lunu Dehi), Salted Lime, 157

R
raisins
    Fancy Yellow Rice (Kaha Bath), 53–55
Rathu Ala Maluwa, 71
red curry, about, 30
red onions. *see* onions, red
rice (bath)
    about, 22
    washing, 42
    Black Pork Curry (Kalu Uru Mas Curry), 119
    Fancy Yellow Rice (Kaha Bath), 53–55
    Ghee Rice (Elagi Thel Bath), 57
    Milk Rice (Kiri Bath), 51
    Rice and Curries Packed in Banana Leaves (Batmula), 61
roti
    Coconut Roti (Pol Roti), 59
    Pol Roti, 59

S
sambol
    about, 45
    Coconut Sambol (Pol Sambol), 152
    Onion Chili Sambol (Lunu Miris Sambol), 153
Sandwiches, Vegetable (Ribbon) Tea, 163
Sauce, Spicy Tomato, 162
scallions

Devilled Prawns (Isso Badthum), 125
screw pine (rampe). *see* pandan/pandanus leaf
seafood
    Crab Curry (Kakuluwo Curry), 131
    Devilled Prawns (Isso Badthum), 125
    Prawn Curry (Isso Curry), 126
Seeni Sambol, 153
slow-cooking methods, 42
Snake Beans (Makaral Thel Dala), Tempered, 87
spices, use of, 34
Spinach (Parippu/Nivithi Parippu), Yellow Dal with/without, 101
spoons, 33
Squash Curry (Wattakka Curry), Winter, 73
stirring techniques, 34
Suthu Ala Curry, 65
Suthu Malu Curry, 127

T
tamarind (siyambala)
    about, 25, 29, 38
    Beef Curry (Harak Mas Curry), 115
tea. *see* drinks
tempering, 42–43
Thakkali Maluwa, 97
Thakkali, Pipinna, Rathu Lunu Salada, 137
tomatoes
    Beef Curry (Harak Mas Curry), 115
    Chicken Curry (Kukul Mas Curry), 111
    Devilled Prawns (Isso Badthum), 125
    Eggplant Salad (Wambatu/Badthala Sambola), 143
    Spicy Tomato Sauce, 162
    Tomato Curry (Thakkali Maluwa), 97
    Tomato, Cucumber, and Red Onion Salad (Thakkali, Pipinna, Rathu Lunu Salada), 137
tuna
    Fried Fish Cutlets (Malu Cutlis), 161

U
Uru Mas Badthum, 121
utensils, 33

V
vangediya, 15
Vel dodan Yusa, 169
vinegar, about, 38

W
walang, 15
Wambatu (Badthala) Curry, 81
Wambatu (Badthala) Sambola, 143
Wambatu Moju, 154
watercress
    Parsley Salad (Parsley
        Sambola), 145
Wattakka Curry, 73

පොලොස් මාළුව.

පොලොස් ගෙඩිය පුංචි කෑලිවලට කපාගෙන. සෝදා ර.ට මිරිස් කුඩු, සරක්කු කුඩු, කහ, ගරන්ඩ දුමා දාලවතී ගනීවා. ඊළඟට.
දෙ පොලොස් ගෙඩියකට, පොල් ගෙඩියක් භාගෙත, රස සාරයක් පමණ එරිකා පොලොස්වලට මිශ්‍රකරමු. වතුර එක්ක එන්න තියා ගෙනත් මාලුට එක්ක ගේන්දර දාලා ර.ට පැය බාගයක් තදු කරමු. මදගින්නේ උදුනක් අමදිව. ර.ට යුදු කපෙ තරම ගස්ම නිසාම වතුර ටිකක්ද තතේ කුඩු දමා ගේයාදා දුර තාගාගනමු.

ගොරහද දෑමක් දෑකම් එතර ගාදු ගාදු පරාවට දාගන

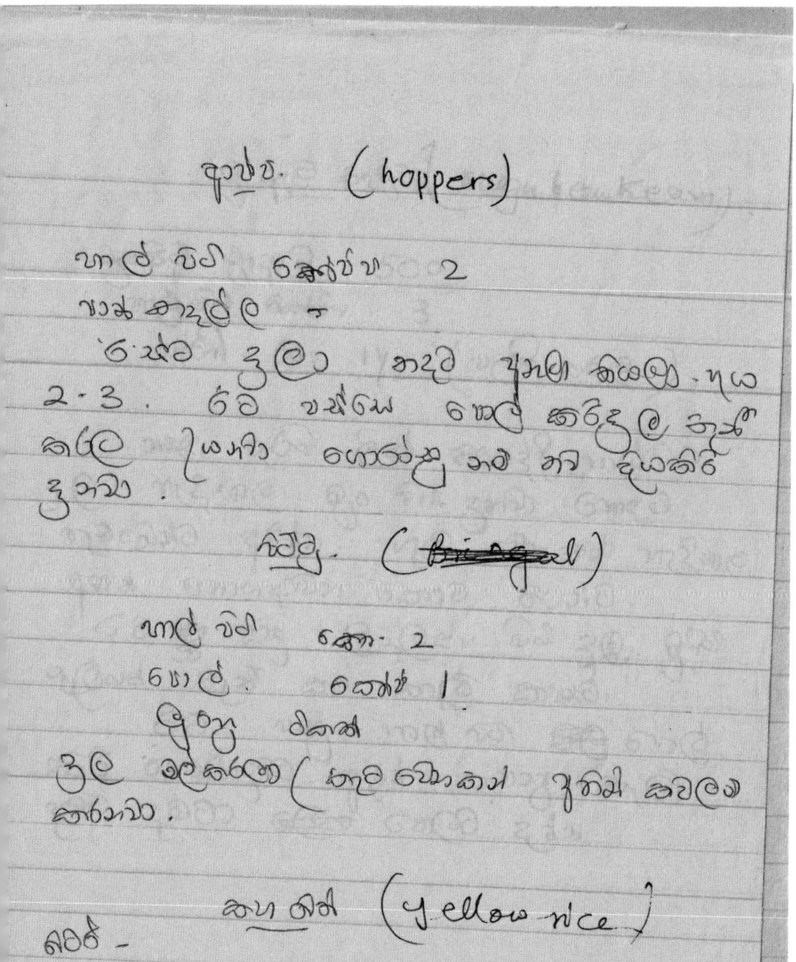

ආප්ප (hoppers)

හාල් පිටි කෝප්ප 2
පාන් පිටි -
යීස්ට් දාලා නාදට අඹ කියලා. තව
2-3 රට වස්සේ තෙල් තරිද්ද ලූනු
කරල් දාලා ගෝස්තු තව නා දියතිරි
දානවා.

රොටී (~~bread~~)

හාල් පිටි කො. 2
පොල් කෝප් 1
ලූනු රසත්
මූල මලකරලා (තුම කොකා දුනිම් කවලා
කරනවා.

කහ බත් (yellow rice)

සරී -
කරවටා, ගිතු රේන, තුරුදුමතු. යොදුර
කරල
ගාලත් බදින තෙර හාල් තුර නැද්ද
තවල මූල යතත් බදිනා. හාල් ලූනු
අහා වතුර ~~බිහා~~ මිශා දනවා.

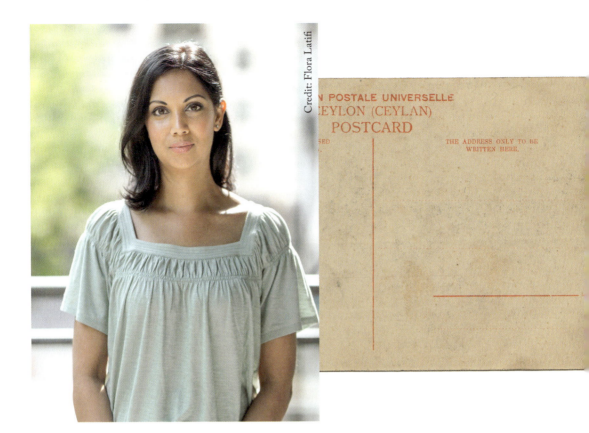

About the Author

While growing up in Canada, Ruwanmali learned about her grandmother's way of cooking, which was typical to her hometown of Kandy, Sri Lanka, from her mother, who exposed her to many ingredients and techniques. Her passion for cooking is inspired by her family's history in farming and gardening. Ruwan's maternal grandfather and uncles worked as agricultural and botanical curators on estates and parks in Sri Lanka's highlands (in Kandy and Nuwara Eliya) and her paternal grandfather owned many fruit, rice, and coconut estates throughout Kandy. Her knowledge of South Asian foods and ingredients has been enhanced by her travels to various parts of Asia and numerous trips to Sri Lanka. She shares her love of her heritage, food, and travel with her husband and daughter.